STUDENT UNIT GUIDE

NEW EDITION

Edexcel A2 Government & Politics
Unit 3C
Representative Processes in the USA

Tremaine Baker

Editors: Eric Magee and Jonathan Vickery

PHILIP ALLAN

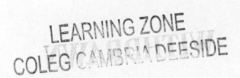

Philip Allan Updates, an imprint of Hodder Education, an Hachette UK company, Market Place, Deddington, Oxfordshire OX15 0SE

Orders

Bookpoint Ltd, 130 Milton Park, Abingdon, Oxfordshire OX14 4SB
tel: 01235 827827
fax: 01235 400401
e-mail: education@bookpoint.co.uk
Lines are open 9.00 a.m.–5.00 p.m., Monday to Saturday, with a 24-hour message answering service.
You can also order through the Philip Allan Updates website: www.philipallan.co.uk

© Tremaine Baker 2012

ISBN 978-1-4441-5298-2

First printed 2012
Impression number 5 4 3 2
Year 2016 2015 2014 2013 2012

Cover photo: Ingo Bartussek/Fotolia

Typeset by Integra, India

Printed in Dubai

Hachette UK's policy is to use papers that are natural, renewable and recyclable products and made from wood grown in sustainable forests. The logging and manufacturing processes are expected to conform to the environmental regulations of the country of origin.

Contents

Content guidance

Questions & Answers

Getting the most from this book

Examiner tips
Advice from the examiner on key points in the text to help you learn and recall unit content, avoid pitfalls, and polish your exam technique in order to boost your grade.

Knowledge check
Rapid-fire questions throughout the Content guidance section to check your understanding.

Knowledge check answers
1 Turn to the back of the book for the Knowledge check answers.

Summary
Summaries
- Each core topic is rounded off by a bullet-list summary for quick-check reference of what you need to know.

Questions & Answers

Exam-style questions

Examiner comments on the questions
Tips on what you need to do to gain full marks, indicated by the icon ⓔ.

Sample student answers
Practise the questions, then look at the student answers that follow each set of questions.

Examiner commentary on sample student answers
Find out how many marks each answer would be awarded in the exam and then read the examiner comments (preceded by the icon ⓔ) following each student answer. Annotations that link back to points made in the student answers show exactly how and where marks are gained or lost.

About this book

This guide is designed to help you revise for Unit 3C Representative Processes in the USA for the Edexcel Advanced (A2) GCE in Government and Politics. This unit looks at the electoral and representative processes of America and considers the extent to which they fulfil the role of popular participation and democracy.

The specification

The four topic areas of Unit 3C are set out below:

Topic	Key coverage
Elections and voting	• Knowledge of the electoral processes used in the USA • Evaluating concerns that elections do not effectively hold those in power to account • Awareness of factors which explain the outcomes of recent elections
Political parties	• Knowledge of the ideologies and traditions of the main parties • Awareness of patterns of support for each party • Evaluation of the changing significance of parties • Exploring the role of minor parties
Pressure groups	• Knowledge of different types of pressure groups and how they access the political system • Exploring how effectively groups are able to influence the political process • Evaluating concerns that pressure groups have a negative impact on the US political system
Racial and ethnic politics	• Knowledge of the extent of, and policies to reduce, racial divisions • Evaluation of the extent of racial and ethnic diversity in the USA, including levels of representation and political activism • Key issues in contemporary minority politics

About this guide

The **Content guidance section** summarises the essential information of Unit 3C including a range of contemporary examples, which are vital to ensure your answers are fully developed and supported. It also includes a range of key terms and a series of examiner tips to help channel your revision into the right areas, plus knowledge checks, which invite you to test various key aspects of your knowledge. These checks are numbered and, at the end of the guide, you can find suggested answers. You can then see how well you did in recalling the key information.

The **Questions & Answers section** includes an array of sample short-answer and essay questions, across all four topics, which are designed to show a range of ability levels. Each answer is followed by a detailed examiner's response which points out what students have done well and also ways in which answers could be improved. You are advised to attempt questions yourself and use this guide to reflect on how you can improve your own responses to potential exam questions.

Content guidance

Elections and voting

At the heart of the American political system is the fundamental fear of tyranny. In this context elections are seen as a crucial way of preventing any group of people, or individual, from becoming politically dominant and using their power oppressively. Thus the overarching feature of this topic is concerned with an evaluation of *how far the political system fulfils its role of holding politicians to account*. There is considerable debate among political commentators about the extent to which the USA is a truly democratic state and how far the frequency, extent and nature of US elections act as a check on power. While many conservatives are quick to point out the relative openness of the system and the range of opportunities for scrutinising and holding politicians to account, more liberal commentators will point to the growth of what they see as a system dominated in particular by money. For these individuals the system is deeply elitist, whereby the wealthy are able to dominate at the expense of the poor, creating a situation in which a growing number of Americans are apathetic, with many choosing not to participate in the political process or even vote.

Because of these concerns the topic also considers arguments about *the extent to which key aspects of the US electoral system are effective and democratic*, as well as *the debate which surrounds possible calls for reform of these elements of the US political system*. In particular, these include debates over:

- the presidential candidate nominating system
- the role of the Electoral College
- the role of campaign finance
- the lack of congressional term limits
- gerrymandering
- low turnout and participation

Fundamental to an understanding of these debates is an understanding of *how the system works*. Students will therefore also be expected to have an understanding of *the key electoral mechanisms in place in the USA*, both in theory and in reality. This topic will guide you through the various stages of the electoral process for the different branches of government.

A final aspect of the topic is an analysis of *the factors which shaped and affected the outcome of the most recent elections*, whether presidential, congressional or midterm, and their significance.

Elitist A description of the idea that political power is held by a small group, or elite. In this book it refers to the idea that certain pressure groups and individuals dominate the political process, due to their wealth or status.

Examiner tip
Specific questions on the outcome of elections will relate to the type of federal election most recently held, either congressional, midterm or presidential. However, more generic questions might refer to the significance of midterms for example, which requires a wider scope of analysis.

Electoral system

The US electoral system reflects the federalist nature of the USA, in which power is held by both state and federal governments. The Founding Fathers, in order to ensure politicians are effectively held to account, created a system in which federal elections are both frequent and fixed, with elections taking place every 2 years. In all these elections a first-past-the-post electoral system is used, whereby a simple majority of votes is required for victory.

Knowledge check 1

What is a federal system of government?

Table 1 Overview of the US electoral system

	Term	Total number	Mechanisms
Legislature: House of Representatives	**2-year** No limit on number of terms	**435** Single-seat districts	• Seats allocated to each state based on the size of the population • Reapportionment of seats undertaken following a census every 10 years • First-past-the-post in all districts
Legislature: Senate	**6-year** No limit on number of terms	**100** State-wide Senate seats	• Every state has two senators • Staggered elections, with one-third being elected every 2 years
Executive: President and vice-president	**4-year** Two-term limit	**2** Elected together on the same ticket	• Indirect election via 538 Electoral College votes • Each state (plus Washington DC) is allocated votes based on population • First-past-the-post winner of a state (except Maine and Nebraska) takes all votes, with 270 votes required to win

House of Representatives

The House term is fixed at 2 years due to its exclusive constitutional powers to initiate money bills, which could open representatives up to corruption. The intention was to create a chamber which is closely aligned to current public opinion, with smaller districts within each state, and which could be tightly scrutinised and regularly held to account for its actions. The numbers of districts in each state are regularly reapportioned, to account for population shifts, and in most states redistricting takes place on a regular basis by the state legislature.

Redistricting The process of redrawing the boundaries of electoral districts to account for population changes within a state. In 36 states this is primarily undertaken by the state legislature.

Senate

The structure of the Senate, in which each state receives two senators regardless of size, is designed to uphold the federalist principles upon which the constitution is based, by protecting the interests of smaller states. In addition to this, the 6-year term and the staggered and state-wide nature of US elections are designed to make the Senate a more contemplative body, cushioned from the vagaries of public opinion.

President

The presidential election is designed to provide a compromise in which the executive office embodies the national will of the USA, while also ensuring that the federalist nature of America and the interests of smaller states are upheld. Thus the president and vice-president are elected together on a single ticket under the Electoral College system. This system indirectly elects the presidential ticket across each of the 50 states, plus Washington DC. Each state is allocated a number of votes in the Electoral College, which is equivalent to the number of seats it has in Congress. Voters in each state do not therefore vote directly for the presidential ticket, but for 'electors' who will choose the president and vice-president in the Electoral College.

The size of the Electoral College is equal to the total membership of Congress (435 representatives and 100 senators) plus the three electors allocated to Washington DC, totalling 538 electors. Therefore, to win the presidency, a candidate must take states worth 270 electoral votes.

Most states, with the exception of Maine and Nebraska, apportion all electors on a first-past-the-post, winner-takes-all system. In this way John McCain won all 11 of Missouri's Electoral College votes in 2008 despite winning by a margin of only 0.13% of the popular vote. The federalist nature of the USA is protected by the fact that all states, regardless of size, have at least three Electoral College votes. Thus small states like Alaska and Vermont had three electors each in 2008, meaning they were significantly over-represented in comparison to more populous states like California, which received 55 electors.

The presidential election day is therefore a series of 51 separate contests in which candidates attempt to win a series of state-based elections in order to secure the magical 270 electors needed to secure victory.

Knowledge check 2

What is the first-past-the-post system?

How are presidential nominations secured?

Due to the fact that the US voter decides who represents the party in the elections, the process to secure the presidency is a long affair. It can, however, be broken down into a number of stages, each of which needs to be successfully negotiated in order for a candidate to become the president of the USA:
- Invisible primary
- Primaries and caucuses
- National conventions
- Presidential debate
- Election day

Invisible primary

This is the stage which runs up to the first formal primary in the USA, effectively beginning as soon as the last election has ended. It is the period when party candidates position themselves to run for the presidency before the formal series of primaries and caucuses starts. During this time the aims of candidates are threefold — to gain media coverage, to gather endorsements and to secure funding.

Media coverage

Candidates will look to achieve widespread name recognition, attempting to gather media airtime and coverage in the printed press. In particular, they will endeavour to present themselves to potential voters as credible presidential candidates and cover any potential weaknesses in their political CV. Thus, following the 2008 election, Sarah Palin, then widely regarded as a possible presidential candidate, looked to strengthen her foreign policy position with trips to both Israel and India in March 2011.

Endorsements

After formal announcements that they are entering the presidential race, candidates will also look to gather support from key individuals within the party. Thus, in the race for the Democratic nomination in 2000, Al Gore made sustained efforts to win over the superdelegate vote, thereby neutralising the threat of his main challenger, former Senator Bill Bradley.

Candidates will also look to gather endorsements from influential groups outside the party who will provide important grassroots support in mobilising a candidate's campaign. For example, 7 months before the first 2012 primary, Michele Bachmann joined almost every other major Republican presidential candidate in speaking at the Faith and Freedom Conference in Washington.

Finance

Perhaps the most important function of this phase is to build up a big enough 'war chest' to fight the long presidential campaign. This is best shown by the withdrawal of ex-Iowa governor Tom Vilsack, who was forced to pull out of the 2008 Democratic race, citing financial difficulties, after a campaign that lasted just 15 weeks. In particular, candidates will look to court key pressure groups and political action committees (PACs) which will provide them with valuable funding. Even those candidates looking to secure federal funding understand the necessity to raise sufficient funds early enough to be able to stay in the race. Although candidates can self-finance their campaigns (as Hillary Clinton did in 2008, spending $11.4 million from her own pocket), it is enormously costly, and very few candidates have the personal assets to do this.

Primaries and caucuses

The first official stage of the presidential election process is the **nomination stage**, which usually takes place between January and June of election year. The key element in this process is the **primary elections**, in which party supporters in each state vote for delegates to go forward to the party convention, which meets to formally select the party's presidential candidate. Each state is awarded party delegates according to the size of the state population.

Candidates who win a state primary or caucus are allocated a certain number, or all, of those state delegates, who are then pledged to vote for that candidate at the national convention. This number depends on whether states allocate their delegates on a proportional or first-past-the-post basis. Thus in Florida in 2008 McCain picked up all 57 of the Republican pledged delegates, despite only beating Mitt Romney by 5%, while in the Democratic race delegates were split, with Clinton picking up 52 and Obama 39.

Superdelegate Key party members, such as governors or mayors, who are sent to the National Party Convention in order to select the party presidential candidate. They are not, unlike other delegates, pledged to vote for a specific candidate.

Federal funding Money supplied to candidates from the public. In the USA, federal 'matching funds' for the primaries match donations made by individual contributors dollar-for-dollar up to a maximum of $250. Major party candidates may also be eligible to receive a federal grant to help fight the general election.

Table 2 Overview of the key primary and caucus events in the nomination stage

Key date/event	Why important?
Iowa caucus	• Traditionally the first result of the process • Widespread news coverage • Seen as an early indication of which candidates might win • Can act as a springboard for candidates, as with Obama in 2008
New Hampshire primary	• Traditionally the first primary result • Widespread news coverage • First major testing ground for candidates • High rate of early dropouts
Super Tuesday (the day on which the greatest number of states hold their primaries)	• More delegates can be won on Super Tuesday than on any other single day • Can 'make or break' candidates • In 2008, it was nicknamed Tsunami Tuesday as so many primaries were held

Examiner tip

The system for electing a party's presidential candidate is very similar to the Electoral College vote. Be careful not to confuse the two. A number of students lose marks each year from a misreading of the question on this area of the topic.

Individual states decide the nature of primaries or caucuses; although there are differences between them, they can roughly be divided into three types. These are compared in more detail in Table 3.

● **Open primaries:** Any registered voter can participate in either the Republican or the Democratic primary, but not both, regardless of the voter's party affiliation. The open primary system is adopted in 16 states, including Texas.

● **Closed primaries:** Only voters who have declared an affiliation to a party can participate in that party's primary. The closed primary system is adopted by 14 states, including New York and Florida.

● **Caucuses:** These are a state-based series of meetings between key party members and supporters, in order to select a party's candidate for the presidency. Caucuses are adopted by 13 states, most notably Iowa.

Table 3 Summary of the advantages and disadvantages of the different systems in the nomination stage

Nomination system	Advantages	Disadvantages
Open primary	• Increases participation, including independent voters • Encourages politicians to have a wider appeal • Usually more moderate voters, filtering out extreme candidates • Good preparation for election	• Can favour candidates with money and a high media profile • 'Raiding' can occur to choose the opposition's weakest candidate • Voters may be ill informed
Closed primary	• Candidates chosen by loyal electorate • Favours candidates with strong grassroots support in the party	• Harder for party outsiders • Lower participation
Caucus	• Favours the well-organised candidate backed by the party • Greater political awareness of electorate	• Low participation and turnout • Candidates may lack wider appeal

Advantages of the nomination process

Democratic

The system is open to the public and actively encourages a much wider voter participation in the selection of candidates. Indeed the increasing use of primaries was a direct result of the McGovern–Fraser reforms, which followed the victory of Hubert Humphrey, who secured the Democratic nomination in 1968 despite standing in no primaries.

The process is also open to any aspiring candidate. In this way, little-known outsider candidates (insurgents), such as Barack Obama in 2008, can rapidly rise to prominence and secure a party's nomination.

Electoral preparation

The primaries are often used as a testing ground for candidates to iron out political campaigns, establish a network of grassroots support and gauge the demands of the electorate. In this way, Obama was able to establish a network of offices across the USA and develop his 'Change we can believe in' campaign before the end of the primary season.

The gruelling nature of the process also narrows the field and eliminates candidates who do not have the political stamina to secure the presidency. Thus it is seen to produce effective candidates, with views which are acceptable to the American people.

Policy debate

The process allows for rival policies to be discussed and debated, enriching the level of political debate across the country. The 2008 primaries included a series of online and televised debates, organised jointly by CNN and YouTube, which pitted the leading candidates from each party against one another.

Disadvantages of the nomination process

Undemocratic aspects

Primaries add a further layer of elections to the process and some argue that the huge number, and frequency, of US elections adds to a growing sense of voter apathy. Indeed despite the unique interest in the Democratic nomination in 2008, turnout at primaries is often below 10%.

Similarly, the primary electorate is unrepresentative of the population, and tends to be older, wealthier and more ideologically partisan, as seen by the relative success of libertarian Republican Ron Paul in 2008.

In addition, the ability of voters to 'raid' opposition primaries is a particular concern in open primaries.

Undermines party control

The lack of party control over the selection process can lead to ill-qualified candidates achieving the nomination, due to a lack of peer review. Thus candidates are chosen based on their personal qualities and campaign skills rather than on their presidential qualities. The introduction of superdelegates to counter this was proven ineffectual

> **Examiner tip**
>
> A possible question is to evaluate how 'effective' or how 'democratic' the nomination process is. Ensure you are aware of the differences in the focus of these questions. The former requires you to focus on how well the process works and if it is successful. The latter requires an evaluation of how open and fair the system is.

in 2008, when Democrat superdelegates were reluctant to support Clinton and go against Obama, who had secured a majority of pledged delegates.

The primary process is also deeply divisive to parties, with the bitter personal battles and inter-party rivalry necessary to secure the nomination.

Frontloading

Frontloading The phenomenon by which states, in order to claim a greater influence on the nominating process, have moved their primaries forward in the election cycle. This leads to a compression of the primary calendar, with many primaries falling into the first 2 months of the process.

The scheduling of primaries has become vital, with a good showing in early primaries considered crucial. Thus the primaries are being compressed (frontloaded) as states compete to be in the early 'make-or-break' rounds. This has two major effects:

- Insufficient time is allowed for adequate debate and reflection time, as candidates with a poor early showing soon drop out. This arguably gives too much prominence to the unrepresentative states of Iowa and New Hampshire.
- Too much importance is attached to raising funds during the invisible primary, which has further lengthened the process by forcing candidates to announce their candidacy earlier. Whereas in 1960 JFK announced his candidacy only 66 days before the first primary, former House Speaker Newt Gingrich announced his candidacy on 11 May 2011 — a clear 278 days before the 2012 Iowa caucus.

Knowledge check 3

Why are Iowa and New Hampshire important events in the presidential nomination process?

Financing focus

The primary process favours those who have raised the biggest 'war chest' in the invisible primary, giving too much weight to money and image rather than issues. It arguably creates a political system dominated by those groups and individuals who are able to secure the most money for candidates, and causes the reality of daily politics in America to be overtaken by the need to raise funds for the next election.

Examiner tip

Questions might ask about the criticisms of the presidential nomination process and possible replacements. Ensure you are able to mention specific reforms which have been suggested to the system, rather than your personal views.

Alternative nominating systems

Although the earlier reforms to the nomination process, which have seen the increasing use of primaries, have been largely welcome, there still exists a level of debate over the need for further reform of the system to improve the democratic nature of primaries. The pressure group FairVote has established a bipartisan 'Fix the primaries' campaign, which aims to examine a range of reform options. These include the following:

Regional primaries

As early as 1999 the National Association of Secretaries of State proposed a plan, similar to a number of other regional plans, which would divide the country up into four regions, each of which would hold primaries on the same day, with the sequence being rotated for which region went first. A variation of this idea is also supported by political analyst Larry Sabato, who referred to the current system as 'a front-loaded mess'. Despite this, some critics claim it would not solve the problem of the cost of elections, due to the fact that a quarter of the country would vote in the first regional set of primaries.

National primaries

In 2007 Jonathan Soros's opinion, as expressed in the *New York Times,* called for the need to establish a system in which all voting in all states takes place on the same day.

Changed scheduling

Other plans have been proposed which would adjust the scheduling of primaries to overcome the problems of frontloading. These include:

- **The American plan:** Small states would begin the primary season, working towards larger states in ten steps, with states chosen at random.
- **The Delaware plan:** This was recommended by a Republican National Committee (RNC) commission in 2000, although rejected by the Republican Party. It relied on 'backloading' primaries, with states placed in four groups according to population size. The smallest states would go first and the largest last.

How is the president elected?

Once the nomination has been achieved, the process for election really kicks off with the national conventions.

National party convention

The traditional role of the national party convention is to formally select the presidential nominee through a vote of pledged delegates and unpledged superdelegates. However, there remains considerable debate about the significance of modern conventions, with some commentators arguing that because of primaries the conventions now merely confirm rather than select the presidential candidate.

Knowledge check 4

What is the difference between a pledged delegate and a superdelegate?

Table 4 The formal and informal roles of the national party convention

Formal roles	Informal roles
Choosing the presidential candidate Formal vote of attending delegates in which the winner must receive an absolute majority of votes	**Restoring party unity** Opportunity to rebuild party unity following the divisive primaries
Choosing the vice-presidential candidate Chosen by the presidential candidate and confirmed by a convention vote	**Enthusing grassroots support** The party faithful are important foot soldiers who need to be galvanised in preparation for the forthcoming election battle
Deciding the party platform Agreement of the policies that the party's candidate intends to pursue if elected	**Exciting the electorate** Conventions are important media events which set out policies and engage ordinary voters, creating a crucial 'bounce' in the polls

Significance

In the formal sense it is arguable that the traditional roles of the party convention are insignificant, and serve no real purpose.

- Conventions are nothing more than a 'rubber stamp', especially given that the party candidate is known in advance. In 2004 John Kerry had secured all but four pledged state delegates, while in 2008 McCain's nearest competitor withdrew his nomination by March.

- Genuine policy debate, to create a party platform, has been replaced by the need for unity. Conventions rarely discuss controversial or divisive policy issues as this can lead to party splits, as with the Republicans in the 1996 convention over abortion. Similarly, the platform is not binding on the president or party members.
- Vice-presidential candidates are now chosen and announced by the presidential candidate in advance of the convention, as with Kerry's choice of John Edwards 3 weeks before the Democratic convention in 2004. However, though often apparent well beforehand, conventions remain an opportunity to present a balanced ticket to the electorate.
- Conventions do play a key role, given the inter-party fighting in primaries, of acting to unify the party. This was most apparent in the need for Clinton and Obama to heal the party wounds from 6 months of continual campaigning.
- There remains the important informal role of presenting a united front to the electorate, which acts as a springboard into the forthcoming election. It gives a post-convention 'bounce' prior to the election campaign — as evidenced, for example, by the Republican grassroots revitalisation and 6% jump in poll ratings following the announcement of the fiscal and social conservative Sarah Palin as the vice-presidential candidate.

Balanced ticket
Choosing a vice-presidential 'running mate' which widens the electoral appeal of the presidential ticket, or counters a perceived policy weakness — for example, Obama chose Joe Biden, the former chair of the Senate Foreign Relations Committee.

Presidential debates

The influence of the media in the presidential election campaign is a much debated subject, with claims that the media are more interested in who is winning — termed 'horse-race' coverage — than in the actual issues. However, the televised presidential debate has come to occupy an important place in the electoral calendar.

Significance

Examiner tip
Questions on the presidential debates are likely to include a need to review both the role and significance of them. Make sure you are able to give specific examples of where they have and have not been significant in recent years.

- Some argue the presidential debate is more about style than substance, encouraging sound-bite politics, with little genuine debate or strong policy lines being adopted by candidates, for fear of alienating important voting groups.
- It is rare for campaigns to turn on the results of presidential debates, although Reagan used the debates well to challenge the incumbent President Carter on his record in 1980, and to address concerns about his age in 1984.
- Presidential debates can be important in encouraging the turnout of the party faithful or turning passive supporters into active voters, as was the case with Kerry in 2004 when Gallup polling showed he closed the 8% gap on President Bush following the debates.
- Viewing figures vary a great deal but there is a generally declining audience. By 2008 this had fallen to around 50 million, although over 73 million tuned into the vice-presidential debate.

What affects the outcome of presidential elections?

Issues

The candidates' policy positions can affect the voting patterns of the electorate and shape the result of the election. Although the election of 2004 was dominated by the 'war on terror' and the war in Iraq, the most common issue is the state of the economy.

Indeed McCain's comment that the 'fundamentals of our economy are strong', in a week of financial crisis, was a significant turning point in the 2008 campaign.

Fundraising

With the increasing cost of campaigns and because very few candidates are able to self-fund campaigns, as Ross Perot did in 1992, the ability to use a range of different methods to secure campaign finances has become a crucial factor in the election. Thus in 2008 Obama became the first major party presidential candidate to reject the federal grant, which would have capped the total amount he was permitted to spend on the election; this allowed him to raise nearly $745 million, which eclipsed the combined candidate total of $646.7 million in 2004.

Campaign strategy

The strength of a campaign is seen as crucial, especially given the Electoral College system (see below) which has created the need for candidates to focus on crucial swing states and voting groups which can affect the outcome. This was shown both by the influence of Karl Rove in 2004, who Bush described as the 'architect' of his victory, and by that of David Axelrod in 2008, who crafted Obama's campaign theme of 'change' as well as his '50-state strategy', forcing McCain to defend previously regarded safe states.

Electoral College system

The final stage in securing the presidency is the general election day, in which candidates attempt to win a majority of **Electoral College** votes (as explained above). This system, designed by the Founding Fathers to indirectly elect the president as a safeguard against 'popular passion', has come under renewed criticism by some in recent years, especially since Bush's victory in the Electoral College in 2000 despite losing the popular vote. However, others are quick to advocate the advantages of the Electoral College system.

Advantages

- **Upholding federalism:** The system protects small state interests, which are over-represented with three electors. Thus candidates must achieve success across all states, as did Obama in 2008 when he won 28 states plus Washington DC.
- **Ensures a strong government:** The system encourages a two-horse race, which usually provides the winner with a secure mandate to govern. Even in the 2000 election, Bush achieved success in 30 states, with 271 Electoral College votes.
- **Ensures widespread support:** Candidates must have depth and breadth of support in order to win. This was shown by Perot's failure to gain sufficient state support in 1992 to win any Electoral College votes. Another example is the limited national support for the pro-segregationist candidate George Wallace in 1968, which meant he failed to win any Electoral College voters outside the South.

Disadvantages

- **Undemocratic:** Too many elements of the system are said to be antiquated and undemocratic, as shown by Al Gore's loss in 2000 and the existence of faithless electors, who ignore the popular vote in their home state.

Swing state Unlike safe states, which almost always vote for either the Democratic or Republican candidate, swing states have no obvious affiliation. They have therefore become known as battleground states, as their electors can be crucial in achieving the 270 Electoral College votes needed.

Faithless elector A member of the Electoral College who does not vote for the winning candidate from their state, who they are pledged to vote for. This was seen in 2000, when Barbara Lett-Simmons, the Washington DC elector, filed a blank vote in protest over lack of congressional representation.

- **Over-representation of small states:** The system causes huge disparities in the level of representation between states, meaning larger states are under-represented. Thus if California were represented on an equal scale to Wyoming it would have 205, rather than 55, electors.
- **Swing states dominate:** Although it prevents populous states from dominating the election, the system does give undue influence to swing states. Thus the elections of 2000 and 2004 hinged on the result in Florida and Ohio respectively. Consequently, these states receive a huge amount of campaign finance and candidate footfall.
- **Minor-party failure:** The system disadvantages minor-party candidates, as seen with Perot's failure to win any electors in 1992 despite polling 18.9% of the vote.
- **Voter apathy:** The existence of safe seats such as Republican Georgia or Democratic California can further encourage low turnout. Voter turnout has consistently averaged around 60% in recent years.

Alternative electoral systems

Although fundamental reform would be very difficult, given that it would require a constitutional amendment which many smaller states or swing states would be reluctant to ratify, many alternatives to the Electoral College system have been proposed. Other than calls for a direct election based on the national popular vote, alternatives include the following:

- **Congressional district method:** This system, which is used in Maine and Nebraska, would allocate electors according to the vote in each congressional district. Thus in Nebraska in 2008 Obama gained one Electoral College vote, even though he lost the overall popular vote in the state; this would not have occurred had Nebraska used a first-past-the-post system. However, this would still not be a proportional system and would have had no impact on the results in 1992, 1996 or 2000.
- **Automatic plan:** This minor reform would automatically allocate state votes, thus preventing the existence of faithless electors.
- **Proportional plan:** This would allocate Electoral College votes in each state proportionally, according to the popular vote. Although this might advantage minor parties, it could make it harder for one candidate to achieve a majority. Fears that it would diminish Colorado's influence in the presidential election led Colorado voters to overwhelmingly reject this system in a 2004 proposition.

Congressional elections

Congressional elections are sometimes dominated by a national agenda, such as with the 1994 Contract with America, or can be overshadowed by the presidential elections. In particular, congressional candidates may benefit from the 'coat-tails effect', where they benefit from the popularity of a presidential candidate, as seen with the Democratic congressional gains in 2008. Usually, however, these elections have a more local focus, with many battles taking place over local matters and the issue of pork barrel politics. The result of this is the creation of a system which massively benefits incumbents, with re-election rates hardly ever falling below 80% for the Senate and only rarely falling below 90% for the House, with the Republican surge of 2010 still witnessing an 85% incumbency rate.

Examiner tip

As well as understanding the different reform proposals, you should also be aware of the strengths and weaknesses of these systems. An easy way to evaluate these is to measure the alternative systems against the advantages and disadvantages of the Electoral College system.

Pork barrel politics
The idea that congressmen focus on channelling government funds into their home state or district. They are thus judged on their success in gaining federal spending projects for 'the folks back home'.

Reasons for incumbency advantage

- **Gerrymandering:** The redrawing of political boundaries to gain a political advantage has created a system whereby very few seats are competitive. Political analyst Charlie Cook's political report claims only 15 House seats will be in the balance in the 2012 elections.
- **Finance:** Incumbents enjoy a huge funding advantage — in 2008, for example, raising three times as much as challengers.
- **Pork barrelling:** Not only do incumbents have specific name recognition, they are also able to point towards a proven track record in benefiting their constituents. Congressman John Murtha became known as the 'king of pork', securing nearly $200 million in 2008.

Midterm elections

As seen in 2010 and on a number of other occasions since the 1990s, there is a growing phenomenon of midterm elections being dominated by a larger national agenda. Midterms, which take place in the middle of a presidential term, are increasingly being seen as a referendum on the president, with the incumbent president's party losing seats in Congress. However, the significance of these elections, given a number of recent results, has been the subject of some debate:

- **1994 Republican revolution:** The Republicans swept to victory with their Contract with America, gaining 54 seats in the House and eight in the Senate.
- **2002:** The midterm elections were held 14 months after 9/11 and saw unusual gains for Bush's party, which picked up ten seats in total.
- **2006:** On the back of the liberal 100-Hour Plan, the Democrats swept to victory by taking control of both the House and the Senate for the first time since 1994.

In this way, although midterms tend to have a lower turnout and profile than presidential elections, they are significant in shaping the national political climate, by pushing issues onto the national agenda, and also in affecting the remainder of a president's term. This has perhaps been best shown in the results and effects of the 2010 midterms.

Results and effects of the 2010 midterms

- **Republican resurgence:** The Tea Party agenda of fiscal conservatism and limited government dominated. Notable victories, such as Marco Rubio securing the Florida Senate seat, show how this became the central issue. Indeed with growing disillusionment among progressive Democrats, feeling that the Obama administration had not gone far enough, and vocal criticism among conservatives of the 'Obamacare' healthcare plan, the Republicans made significant gains. Although the six Senate seats were not enough to gain a majority, they did pick up 63 House seats.
- **Referendum on Obama:** With discontent over healthcare and economic stimulus, Obama has been forced to adopt a more compromising tone, as did Bill Clinton following the 1994 Republican revolution.
- **Gridlock:** Republicans have been emboldened to be more uncompromising and forceful, as seen with the extension of Bush tax cuts in 2010 and in achieving a tough federal budget cut of $38 billion in 2011.

Examiner tip

There is considerable crossover between topics in this unit, for example with the detail on the Contract with America and the 100-Hour Plan falling into the parties section. If you struggle to retain knowledge, try to focus on examples which can be used across a range of topics and may be useful with different exam questions.

Direct democracy

Direct democracy, in which decisions are made directly by the people rather than by the federal government, is undertaken in many US states. Some states allow for voters to petition legislatures to directly remove elected officials, under **recall** election procedures, and also to veto a state bill, under procedures for calling a **referendum**. However, by far the most common and effective method is the use of propositions, or **initiatives**, as seen by the widespread ballot measures voted on in the 2010 midterms. These included the banning of affirmative action in Arizona Proposition 107 and attempts to limit the rights of federal government to fine state citizens for not taking up health insurance in Oklahoma and Arizona.

> **Proposition** A state-based initiative by which voters can force a public vote on an issue by obtaining a petition signed by a certain minimum number of registered voters.

Advantages of propositions

- **Controversial subjects** which state legislatures are reluctant to tackle can be voted on, as with the attempted legalisation of marijuana in California Proposition 19.
- Propositions can **increase participation** and turnout, as seen with the conservative propositions placed on the ballot in many swing states in 2004 to try and increase the Republican vote, such as the Ohio proposition to ban same-sex marriages.
- Propositions **increase accountability** of politicians, who are forced to be responsive to voter demands, such as Florida's 2008 ban on gay marriage.
- They **engage the electorate**, who become better informed and are encouraged to join pressure groups in response. In 2010, all six Colorado propositions were defeated by the electorate, including attempts to severely restrict abortion.

Disadvantages of propositions

- They can be **inflexible** and undermine the principles of a representative democracy by tying the hands of state legislatures. In this way California Proposition 13, which prevented property tax from being raised, has limited politicians' ability to tackle the spiralling budget deficit.
- They can be **manipulated by wealthy groups**, as seen by the hiring of public relations firm Schubert Flint to run the successful Proposition 8 campaign, which saw the ban on same-sex marriages in California.
- A **tyranny of the majority** is created by disadvantaging minority groups, for example the effect of California Proposition 209 on African Americans and 187 on Latinos.

> **Examiner tip**
> With this topic, ensure you do not confuse US propositions, which originate from citizens and affect states laws, with UK referendums, which originate from Parliament and affect national laws. It is best to avoid answering proposition questions by adapting AS questions on UK referendums.

Concerns about the US electoral system

There remains considerable debate over the extent to which US elections hold politicians to account. This has led to the passage of a number of reforms which have attempted to restrict funding, along with a number of other proposed reforms, which some commentators have suggested are necessary to make the system fairer.

Funding

The system of generating campaign finance, which tends to benefit incumbents or wealthy individuals, as well as the increasing cost of electoral campaigns, has led to calls for greater restrictions on campaign finance. The problem has been in securing reform which strikes a balance between creating a fair playing field and not impinging on democratic rights to freedom of expression.

Table 5 Summary of the key campaign finance reforms

Reform	Key terms	Effects
Federal Election Campaign Act 1974 (FECA)	• Limited expenditure of candidates • Provided federal 'matching funds' • Limited the amount individuals and corporations could donate	• *Buckley* v *Valeo* (1976) struck down any limits on candidate expenditure, unless the candidate accepts public financing • Saw the rise of political action committees (PACs) to circumvent restrictions on donations
FECA amendment 1979	• Allowed parties to raise and spend money	• Rise of '**soft money**' funding, which is money not openly given to a candidate's campaign but which is given to parties which are able to use it to assist a candidate's election
Bipartisan Campaign Reform Act 2002 (BCRA)	• Abolished 'soft money' • Increased individual contribution limit • Restricted non-party advertisements which identify a federal candidate	• Proliferation of 527s, raising money as 'independent' groups • *Citizens United* v *FEC* (2010) overturned advertising restrictions, allowing corporations and unions to promote a candidate. This has seen a rise of Super PACs with unrestricted spending

Despite these reforms, the cost of elections continues to escalate, with 2008 being the first ever $1 billion election. Obama declined public funds and generated huge amounts from small (less than $250) internet donations, meaning he was able to raise almost half of McCain's total expenditure in the month of September alone.

Examiner tip
Campaign finance will not be the sole subject of essay questions. However, you should understand the reasons for and consequences of campaign finance reforms, which may well be a short-answer question and specifically links to the pressure groups topic.

Congressional term limits

The huge incumbency advantage has led some political commentators, like Lawrence Lessig, to compare Congress to the communist Politburo in terms of length of tenure. Similarly, congressmen are criticised for being so fixated on re-election that they have become overly concerned with developing relations with key donors and pork barrel politics. This has led to calls, from groups such as the Heritage Foundation, for congressional term limits, similar to the presidency (see Table 1, page 7). Calls for term limits were particularly high with the Republican revolution of 1994, but the idea was never fully pursued, and has not gained much momentum since.

Gerrymandering

In most states, because the redrawing of political boundaries is undertaken by state legislatures, it has led to widespread claims that the system is open to abuse from unfair partisan gerrymandering. Examples such as the Maryland 4th district and the

LEARNING ZONE
COLEG CAMBRIA DEESIDE

Bipartisan Refers to a
political system in which
two opposing parties
seek to compromise
their political positions
in order to reach a
shared agreement on
policy matters. In this
way parties govern
through cooperation and
negotiation rather than
opposition and adversity.

Knowledge check 5

What are the election
cycles for the House of
Representatives, Senate
and presidency?

Illinois 4th '**earmuff district**', connecting two Latino areas by a thin strip of land,
have been criticised as a manipulation of the electoral system. Many states, such as
California following the approval of Proposition 20 in 2010, have handed control to
a bipartisan redistricting committee. Indeed groups such as FairVote have called
for Congress to pass a Redistricting Act, which would require state legislatures to
appoint independent commissions.

Participation

Turnout in US elections is one of the lowest of any western democracy, with turnout for
midterms rarely rising above 50%. There is ongoing debate as to the reasons for this.

- **The first-past-the-post system,** along with the use of **gerrymandering,**
  creates safe seats in which a vote for certain party candidates is wasted. A system
  in which huge numbers of votes are not counted discourages people from voting.
- **The frequency of elections,** which often take place all year round for various
  local, state and national posts, can lead to voter apathy. Similarly, the increasing
  length of election cycles, especially with the addition of invisible primaries due
  to frontloading, can lead to electoral boredom.
- **Registration procedures** are difficult and present a further barrier to voting.
  Attempts have been made to simplify the process, for example with the 1993
  Motor Voter Act, which allowed citizens to register to vote when applying for a
  driving licence. However, estimates suggest that universal voter registration would
  increase turnout only by between 8 and 10%.
- **The electorate's perceptions** are important, with some highlighting how the
  system produces a lack of choice and the idea that the system is controlled by a
  wealthy elite with little hope for ordinary voters to change the system. Indeed, with
  turnout being less than 40% among the poorest fifth of the population, there is
  some weight to this argument.

Advocates for reform of the system thus propose an array of measures to tackle the
problem. However, the main suggestion is for the implementation of a more proportional
electoral system, such as national popular vote (NPV), followed by instant runoff voting
(IRV) or preferential voting.

Knowledge summary

- Knowledge and understanding of the various
  electoral processes in place in the USA, including
  those of primaries, presidential candidate selection,
  presidential and congressional elections and those
  which allow direct democracy to take place.
- Ability to critique these processes by evaluating the
  benefits and drawbacks of each of the mechanisms
  used in the US electoral system.
- An understanding of the factors which have affected
  the outcome of recent federal elections, with
  particular focus given to the most recent election
  held.

- Ability to evaluate the extent to which US elections
  hold politicians to account, and the reasons for
  criticisms of the existing system, and possible
  reforms of it.
- Awareness of the criticisms of, and alternatives
  to, aspects of the system, including the Electoral
  College, presidential candidate nomination system,
  campaign finance, congressional term limits,
  gerrymandering, and low voter turnout.

Political parties

Unlike their British counterparts, American parties have traditionally been seen as broad, non-ideological coalitions representing a number of regional and sectional interests. Students should be aware of the strong thread of localism and regionalism which runs through the US political system, due to the decentralised nature of the federalist system and the relative independence of state-based party structures.

The first aspect of this topic is therefore concerned with *the extent to which US political parties have become more ideologically cohesive* in their values and policies. While many scholars agree that there is a trend towards a much greater ideological polarisation of the two main parties, in recent years the relative influence of the different factions within each party has been the subject of much debate among political commentators.

This debate about the ideological polarisation of the main political parties has also led some commentators to suggest that there has been an overall resurgence in the importance, and power, of political parties within the US political system. These political commentators point towards the growing centralisation of US parties, as a result of the use of soft money financing and the increasing powers of party leaders to effectively choose congressional committee chairs, as evidence of this rising party power. In contrast, other commentators have argued that the role and functions of political parties have been undermined by other bodies, such as pressure groups, meaning they are in serious, if not terminal, long-term decline. They suggest that the powers of US party leaders are constrained by both the candidate-centred, regional nature of the US political system and by their relative inability to influence candidate selection due to the proliferation of party primaries since the 1970s.

A third area to consider is the *impact of these shifts on the traditional support base* of each party. Although it is hard to pinpoint a 'typical' Republican or Democrat voter, there are certain historical and contemporary factors which shape the voting patterns of particular groups. Thus students will be expected to understand which groups tend to vote for each party and the reasons for this support.

The final area in this topic is the nature of the party system itself, and *the factors which have limited the success of minor parties* and given the two main parties such a dominant position in the US political system. Although there are numerous obstacles to minor-party success, especially electorally, there is a requirement for students to engage in a political discussion about the extent of minor-party impact at both a local and national level, and particularly in congressional and presidential elections.

Historical context

For much of America's history the main parties were little more than loose coalitions of individuals serving the interests of a range of groups in society. In this context, the main parties have often been referred to as **'umbrella' parties**. However, a number of key events have helped shape the current positions of both the Democratic and Republican parties.

Polarisation The process by which party ideologies and political opinions have become increasingly divided, whereby the views of moderates are overshadowed by the more extreme views and factions in a political party. Thus the rise of the fiscally conservative Tea Party Republicans has arguably shifted the Republican Party further to the right of the political spectrum.

'Umbrella' parties The idea that the decentralised nature of US politics has led to weak party structures in which both main parties encompass a broad range of ideologies and groups within them which are very loosely united under the banner of one party.

New Deal Coalition

Prior to the Great Depression, the support base of the Democratic Party traditionally came from the **Solid South** — white supporters in the southern states who largely rejected the Republican Party due to its role in the civil war and support for the abolition of slavery. It also included recent immigrants, such as those from the Irish and Italian communities, who were mainly based in northern cities.

However, following the establishment of the New Deal by President F. D. Roosevelt in the 1930s, the Democratic Party widened its support base to include a number of new groups. These included blue-collar workers, who benefited massively from the range of government-funded programmes established under the New Deal and the protections it introduced for trade unions; and various minority groups, especially the poorer racial and ethnic minorities, who benefited from the increasing benefits and jobs created by the programme.

Breaking the Solid South

The 1960s saw a realignment of the party positions following the Democratic support for the Civil Rights movement in the 1950s and 1960s, and the exploitation of this by the Republicans. The Democrats in the South, previously regarded as pro-segregationists, saw their dominance eroded by the Republican 'Southern Strategy' adopted by Richard Nixon, which actively targeted the conservative states in the South.

Recent ideological partisanship

These historical events have arguably produced a more polarised party system, in which the Democrats seem to have become the party of the liberal left, while the Republicans have become more clearly that of the conservative right.

A number of commentators point towards the highly partisan nature of US politics today, with many blaming the threats of government closure in 2011, over federal budget cuts, on the loss of a spirit of compromise which had previously been seen in Washington. Many people point towards the fact that moderate views within the Republican Party have been sidelined, as shown by McCain's choice in 2008 of Sarah Palin as his running mate in order to appeal to the fiscal and socially conservative heart of the party. Similarly, the loss of many conservatives from the Democratic Party, whose numbers in the House fell by over half in the 2010 midterms, shows how the party has become increasingly dominated by those on the left. Indeed there is a wealth of evidence supporting this notion of a growing party polarisation in America. Many now claim that the USA is a politically divided society, in which the Republicans have become a largely right-wing conservative party in stark contrast to the more left-wing liberal Democratic Party.

Conservative Republicans

Since the Republican resurgence in the 1994 midterm elections, in which the Republicans promoted their Contract with America, the Republican Party has moved more sharply to

---

Examiner tip

With any question about the ideological divisions between the two main parties, make sure that you focus on the *current positions* of the parties with recent examples and evidence. Dated examples, though given some reward, will not show the examiner your ability to fully evaluate and judge the contemporary positions of the two parties.

Partisan An adversarial political system, in which parties compete for power and hold sharply different ideologies. In this system politicians from one party wholeheartedly support their party's policies and are often reluctant to acknowledge the accuracy of their political opponents' views.

Knowledge check 6

What are midterm elections?

---

the right. The nationally agreed manifesto committed party members to vote on a series of conservative issues, such as anti-crime measures. This was further entrenched by the activities of Newt Gingrich, then House Speaker, to enforce a greater degree of party discipline in Congress through the actions of party whip Tom 'The Hammer' DeLay; and with the implementation of the K Street Project, which attempted to increase the number of conservative PACs (Political Action Committees) and lobbyists in Washington. Further evidence of the dominance of conservatives within the Republican Party can be found in the following:

Examiner tip

Exam questions will often focus on the extent to which there are ideological differences between the two main parties. You should therefore look to provide evidence for both sides of the argument. Without this balanced examination of the arguments, regarding similarities and differences between the parties, you will fail to pick up many synoptic or evaluative marks.

- Despite advocating 'compassionate conservatism', George W. Bush's period in office saw him adopt a socially conservative stance on many key issues. Examples include his veto of stem cell research bills and suspension of federal funding for family planning groups which performed or promoted abortion services.
- There has been an increasingly strong anti-spending focus within the party, as seen by the fact that in January 2009 Obama's press for an economic stimulus package saw every single House Republican vote against it.
- The Republicans universally opposed the Democrats' 2010 Healthcare Act, with all 178 Republicans in the House opposing the final passage of the bill.
- There have been many instances of more moderate Republicans facing well-funded and well-organised conservative challengers in their primaries. Indeed the Tea Party movement deliberately targeted moderate Republicans in the 2010 midterms, unseating incumbents such as Alaska's Lisa Murkowski, or popular front-runners such as Florida governor Charlie Crist.
- The 2009 special congressional election for New York's 23rd district saw conservative Republicans back the New York Conservative Party candidate over their own Republican candidate, Dede Scozzafava, on the charge that she was too liberal on a host of issues including government spending and abortion rights.
- Prior to the 2010 midterms, conservative members of the Republican National Committee also implemented a 'purity' resolution, which proposed a ten-point conservative ideological platform and required GOP candidates to adhere to at least eight of these in order to secure party funding. This included the commitment to oppose 'Obama-style government-run healthcare'. The party similarly drafted a 'Pledge to America' commitment of legislative priorities it would look to tackle upon assuming office.

Liberal Democrats

The Democrats, in contrast, have arguably adopted a more liberal agenda and policy position on many economic and social issues, such as those regarding government intervention and abortion. Evidence of this shifting position can be seen from the following:

- In 2006 the Democrats wrested control of the House and Senate from the Republicans with a clearly liberal **100-Hour Plan.**
- In one of his first measures as president, Obama reinstated federal funding for international family planning groups which promote or provide advice about abortions.
- The Democrats passed the 2009 economic stimulus plan on largely partisan lines, with only 11 House Democrats voting against it; while many in the party led the unsuccessful attempts to prevent the extension of Bush tax cuts to more wealthy Americans in 2010.

100-Hour Plan

The commitment by Democrats to use the first 100 hours of legislative time in Congress to pass a number of liberal measures. These included the establishment of affordable healthcare and the raising of the minimum wage.

- A number of Democrats have faced well-organised opposition from liberal groups through the party primaries. The most noteworthy was the 2006 defeat of Joe Lieberman by Ned Lamont. Similarly, Senate incumbent Blanche Lincoln of Arkansas fought off a fierce primary challenge in 2010 from party liberals angered by her opposition to a government-run 'public option' as part of the healthcare reform law.
- The **2010 Healthcare Act**, which expanded insurance coverage to over 30 million Americans, was part of the liberal healthcare reform agenda of the 111th Congress. Its passage was deeply partisan, with all Republicans, and only 34 Democratic representatives, voting against it.
- In December 2010 the Democrat-controlled Congress repealed the controversial 'Don't ask, don't tell' policy, which prohibited openly gay persons from serving in the military. In the vote every single Democrat senator voted for the repeal.

Party factions and bipartisanship

Despite considerable evidence of an increasing partisanship, both parties still have a number of core factions which serve to influence and shape the policy directions of the party in some way. Indeed the regional diversity of America, and the increasing use of primaries to select candidates, mean that the practical considerations of winning elections lead both sides to retain a broader ideological base. This is partly in order to win over the political centre ground, while also appealing to the individual ideological positions of the electorate in the various states and congressional districts across America. As a result, both parties include a range of factions, which compete for influence within the party.

Republican Party factions

There are three main factions within the Republican Party.

Fiscal conservatives

This group advocates free-market economics, a minimalist governmental approach to the economy and a balanced federal budget. Fiscal conservatives specifically promote a programme of reducing both business and personal taxation, moderating the regulation of businesses and cutting government expenditure. The influence of this faction within the party has most recently been evidenced by the rise of the Tea Party Caucus in both the House and the Senate. This group adopted deeply entrenched views during the 2011 budget negotiations over the issue of raising the US debt ceiling, to secure a $38 billion cut in federal spending. Leading members of this faction include:

- Republican presidential hopeful **Michele Bachman**, who won the 2011 Iowa straw poll just 2 months after announcing her candidacy
- Texan Representative **Ron Paul**, the influential Republican with libertarian views, who is running for the presidential nomination again in 2012
- congressional newcomers, brought in on what has been described as the 'Tea Party tidal wave' of 2010, including Senators **Rand Paul** and **Marco Rubio**

Examiner tip
Stronger students will be expected to give detailed and specific examples of the various factions and their influence on the policy direction of each party. Simply identifying that a Northern Democrat differs from a Southern Democrat, or that both parties are broad-church organisations with a range of ideologies within them, will get limited credit.

Libertarian The idea that individual liberty is the central factor which any government should look to uphold. It thus involves the belief that individuals should be given the maximum personal and political liberty, while government should minimise its involvement in people's lives.

Social conservatives

Often referred to as the 'religious right', this faction encompasses a range of Christian political groups which advocate a set of deeply conservative social policies. These include opposition to abortion, same-sex marriage and stem cell research. Indeed the increasing influence of the social conservatives within the party is best evidenced by the comments of former Senator Arlen Spector, following his 2009 defection to the Democratic Party, when he said that the 'Republican Party has moved farther and farther to the right'. Many members of the party have been forced to adopt a more orthodox conservative stance on these issues in a bid to secure the party's nomination for president, notably Mitt Romney and John McCain. Leading members of this faction include:

- House Speaker **John Boehner**, who claimed the No Taxpayer Funding for Abortion Act, part of the Republican 'Pledge to America', which was passed by the House in May 2011, was one of the 'highest legislative priorities' of the 112th Congress.
- Darling of the right, **Sarah Palin**, whose choice as vice-presidential candidate in the 2008 election race shot her to prominence. However, since then she has remained a prominent advocate for the Tea Party movement, despite not holding elective office, and was influential in promoting a number of social and fiscal conservative candidates in the 2010 midterms.
- **Rick Perry**, running for the Republican nomination for president in 2012, who in his role as Texas governor has signed into law a number of bills which have served to severely limit abortions in the state, including the abolition of state funding for abortion providers.

Moderates

The Republican moderates tend to adopt a less conservative view towards many aspects of social and fiscal policy. The faction has become known as the Main Street Partnership, because of its more moderate and centrist views. The influence of the moderates, however, previously a dominant force in the party, has arguably declined in recent years. This is perhaps best evidenced by the fact that John McCain, despite winning the 2008 nomination, struggled to secure funding from many conservative groups, especially following their criticism of his liberal stance over immigration and support for a 2007 bill to provide illegal immigrants with a path to citizenship. It was not until McCain appeared to adopt a more conservative stance on these matters, and particularly by choosing Sarah Palin as his vice-presidential candidate, that he was able to galvanise Republican grassroots supporters and key conservative donors to his presidential electoral bid. Other members of the moderate faction include:

- Maine Senators **Olympia Snowe** and **Susan Collins**, who have given a degree of support to both legalised abortions and gay rights. They were two of only eight Republican senators to vote in favour of the repeal of the 'Don't ask, don't tell' policy.
- Pennsylvania Representative **Charlie Dent**, who since 2007 has been co-chair of the Republican Tuesday Group, a group of moderates who meet weekly to discuss mutual policy priorities. Despite conservative successes in the 2010 midterms, this group claimed 49 Republican moderate members in 2011, its highest level since it was founded following the 1994 Republican revolution.

Knowledge check 7

Name three specific moderate or conservative factions within the Republican Party.

Democratic Party factions

Similar to the Republicans, there are three main factions in the Democratic Party:

Liberal activists

This faction consists of a broad range of members who are committed to a more progressively liberal agenda. This would include defending those rights which are seen to be most threatened by the conservative right: advocating wider healthcare provision, as well as upholding a range of rights for gay people, racial minorities and women, specifically abortion. The rising influence of the liberal activists within the party has best been shown by the success of the liberal 100-Hour Plan and the 6 for '06 agenda, which saw the Democrats sweep to power in the midterm elections of that year. Similarly, despite heavy losses in the 2010 midterms, the Congressional Progressive Caucus remains the biggest faction among House Democrats, with 75 members. Prominent Democratic progressives include:

- House Minority Leader **Nancy Pelosi**, who was a founding member of the Congressional Progressive Caucus and key architect of the 6 for '06 agenda. Since then she has been instrumental in the passage of the 2007 Fair Minimum Wage Act, the 2009 Economic Stimulus package and the 2010 Healthcare Act.
- Senator **Sherrod Brown**, who was judged to be one of the *National Journal*'s 'most-liberal senators' of both 2009 and 2010. He has been a strong advocate of equal rights for gay people, including support for both gay marriage and adoption.
- President **Barack Obama**, who, during his short tenure as a senator, was reported as being the most liberal senator of 2007. Since becoming president, he has overseen attempts to close down Guantanamo Bay, albeit unsuccessfully, and has proposed a host of liberal policies to Congress including the healthcare and fiscal stimulus plans.

Moderates

The roots of this modern-day faction lie in Democratic attempts to win back the White House under Bill Clinton, and in the establishment of the centrist Democratic Leadership Council. In this way the moderates adopted a more pragmatic approach to policy development, which attempted to appeal to both the conservative heartland of America and the more progressive elements of society. In its current form the most prominent congressional group is the New Democrat Coalition (NDC), which, as of 2011, retained 42 House Members. Though the moderates appeared to lose influence following Al Gore's loss in the 2000 presidential election and the subsequent rise of progressives within the party, they still have a moderating influence on the party, especially since the loss of the House in the 2010 midterms and the subsequent need for greater compromise and bipartisanship. Key figures include:

- Secretary of State **Hillary Clinton**, who was a former member of the Senate NDC and, while senator for New York, supported military action in both Afghanistan and Iraq.
- Democratic Party affiliate **Joe Lieberman**, who successfully ran as an independent following his loss in the 2006 party primary to progressive-sponsored Ned Lamont. Despite adopting conservative positions on foreign and defence policy, he was a vocal supporter of the repeal of the 'Don't ask, don't tell' policy.

- Arizona Representative **Gabrielle Giffords**, who is a member of both the New Democrat and Blue Dog coalitions and describes herself as 'working for fiscally conservative, pro-business economic policies'. Despite being a strong advocate of gun rights she is pro-choice on abortion.

Conservatives

This is the most right-wing faction within the Democratic Party. Although encompassing a broad set of ideologies, conservative Democrats are on the whole in favour of reducing taxes and adopting a conservative approach to social policies, which respects traditional Christian values. Their numbers grew hugely following the 2006 Democrat electoral victories. They have since achieved considerable success in watering down the eventual 2010 Healthcare Act, through securing withdrawal of proposals for a government public insurance option and by obtaining a commitment from Obama to introduce an executive order banning federal funding of abortions in return for their support. However, recent commentators have suggested that following the loss of over half their number in the 2010 midterms, which has left them with just 25 members, they are a dying breed. Indeed the announcement of the retirement of at least two other prominent Blue Dogs, and the fact that redistricting for 2012 is likely to lead many of those remaining to be vulnerable to Republican challengers, shows the degree to which they are a declining influence within the party. Current conservative Democrats include:

- Georgia Representative **John Barrow**, who is a leading member of the Blue Dog Coalition. He was one of the 34 representatives who voted against the 2010 Healthcare Act.
- Nebraska Senator **Ben Nelson**, who describes himself as a having 'strong pro-life beliefs' and was deemed the most conservative Democratic member of the Senate in 2010 by both the *National Journal* and the American Conservative Union.

Party decline or party renewal?

The claim by one political commentator at the beginning of the 1990s that 'parties are in full retreat' shows the key debate for this topic, which centres on how far parties have retained power and influence within the American political system. Some commentators point towards the changing role of parties, which has led to a decline in their key traditional roles: selecting candidates, fundraising, communicating with the electorate and developing policy. However, others have suggested a renewal of party power, given that they still retain a large degree of control over these areas and have developed a stronger leadership, along with a greater degree of partisanship and coordination, in recent years.

Evidence of party decline

Primaries

The increasing use of primaries in selecting candidates has given less power to party leadership to shape the direction of the party. This was best seen by the successful Tea Party infiltration of some Republican target seats in 2010, which were eventually

Knowledge check 8

What is the difference between pro-life and pro-choice views?

Executive order A legally binding directive given to the federal bureaucracy by the US President. These orders state how federal agencies and officials should interpret congressionally established laws or policies. They thus allow presidents to guide and direct the implementation of congressional laws.

Knowledge check 9

Name at least five specific factions in each of the two main parties.

lost to Democrats. In this way, Christine O'Donnell won the Republican primary for the Delaware Senate seat only to go on to lose the election by a margin of 17%.

Furthermore, the divisive nature of primaries encourages inter-party rivalry. Indeed the battle between Clinton and Obama for the 2008 Democratic presidential nomination showed how deeply divisive they can be.

Limits on funding

Limits on party fundraising and expenditure have been introduced by the recent campaign finance laws. These have allowed presidential candidates to secure federal funding independent of the parties. Also, the 2002 BCRA (Bipartisan Campaign Reform Act) placed a ban on soft money.

Pressure groups

Pressure groups have replaced parties in communicating with the electorate, mobilising voters and developing policy. The rise of 527 groups and Super PACs, which are proliferating because of their ability to collect unlimited amounts of money, is one example of this. The Super PAC 'Make Us Great Again', set up by Rick Perry's former chief of staff, was quick to campaign in favour of his candidacy for the Republican presidential nomination just weeks after his announcement to run. Similarly, other groups have been established, such as the NRA Political Victory Fund and Moveon.org, to mobilise the electorate and encourage them to vote for certain candidates at election time. Finally, pressure group 'think tanks' are also increasingly undertaking policy development and exerting influence on the policy direction of the main parties. In this way, the liberal Centre for American Progress has been claimed to be the keystone of the Obama administration, and a *Time* magazine article from 2008 claimed that 'not since the Heritage Foundation helped guide Ronald Reagan's transition in 1981 has a single outside group held so much sway'.

Evidence of party renewal

Control over the nomination process

The parties have attempted to recapture the nomination process through the introduction of superdelegates, although the degree of influence they exert, in comparison to pledged state delegates, is debatable. However, the close 2008 Democratic presidential primary race did lead *The Guardian* to refer to the 795 superdelegates as the 'most powerful people in American politics'.

In addition, party control over the nomination procedures has been upheld in a series of Supreme Court rulings regarding the timing of primaries, as highlighted by the disqualification of Florida and Michigan in 2008 for violating Democratic Party rules.

Party structure and leadership

The parties have developed national party structures and leadership since the 1970s, which has served to strengthen their position. In particular, the Brock reforms led to the establishment of a permanent headquarters for the Republican National Committee.

Examiner tip

Evidence of party renewal can also be found in the greater degree of partisanship among the two main parties. Therefore, in your essay answers you need to spend time reviewing the degree to which the parties are similar and different and how accurate it is to refer to the Democrats as 'liberal' and the Republicans as 'conservative' (see earlier headings).

Fundraising involvement

Parties are still involved in important fundraising activities, particularly through the establishment of various campaign committees to assist the election of party candidates. In this way, the Democratic Senatorial Campaign Committee spent over $129 million, and the National Republican Senatorial Committee $68 million, on the 2010 midterms.

Control of the political agenda

Greater coordination of the party in Congress has given more power to the party leadership to control the political agenda. In particular, the House Speaker has increasingly managed to dominate the selection of committee chairs and membership, which was utilised by Newt Gingrich and Nancy Pelosi respectively following the 1994 and 2006 midterms.

Party support

With the increasing partisanship of American politics seen from the 1990s onwards, some commentators were arguing that the electorate itself has become more and more polarised. With this in mind, it is possible to identify certain voting trends and groups which are inclined to vote for the Republican or Democratic Party. These are set out in Table 6 and Table 7.

Republican Party support

Table 6 Summary of Republican Party support (including % vote according to the CNN News exit poll of the 2008 presidential election)

Group	Reasons for support
High-income business professionals, with income over $100,000 (51%)	• Republican fiscal conservative views have always been appealing to this group • During the 2010 negotiations over the extension of Bush-era tax cuts, the Democrats unsuccessfully attempted to abolish the lower rate of taxation for those earning over $250,000 against considerable Republican opposition
White southerners (54%)	• The historic breaking of the Democrat Solid South, over black civil rights, has created a Republican stronghold in this area • This dominance is linked to the success of the Republican Southern Strategy, which targeted disaffected white southerners, and to the high degree of church attendance in many of these 'bible belt' states (see Protestant Christian groups below)
Rural voters (53%)	• Many favour the limited government regulation supported by the Republicans and especially their general opposition to gun control • This was evidenced by the massive rise in gun sales reported within a week of Obama winning the presidential election in 2008 because of fears of further restrictions among gun owners

Examiner tip

If a question asks about which groups tend to vote for a particular party, and why, make sure that your answer relates to specific groups and their motives for voting in a certain way. Use specific examples of policies which these groups would find appealing. No reward will be given to a review of party factions or policies which are not related to voting groups.

Group	Reasons for support
Protestant Christians (54%)	• They support the traditional moral values espoused by socially conservative Republicans • This would include their opposition to abortion, as seen by the House Republicans' overwhelming support for a measure to cut off federal funding to pro-abortion group Planned Parenthood in 2011 • It was a Republican-controlled Congress which passed the Defence of Marriage Act in 1996, preventing the federal government from recognising same-sex marriage
White males (57%)	• Many white males tend to prefer the Republican position on social policies • They are particularly opposed to the support among many Democrats for affirmative action • This was clearly shown by the 2004 Democratic platform, which professed support for 'affirmative action to redress discrimination', which many white males argue is reverse discrimination

Democratic Party support

Table 7 Summary of Democratic Party support (including % vote according to the CNN News exit poll of the 2008 presidential election)

Group	Reasons for support
Low-income working class, with income under $30,000 (60%)	• Many are unionised members who favour the more interventionist approach of the Democratic Party • The Fair Minimum Wage Act 2007, raising the federal minimum wage from $5.15 to $7.25 per hour, shows the party's commitment to this low-earning group
Gays and lesbians (70%)	• They favour the Democrats' more liberal stance on social policies, and general commitment to gay rights • In a recent press release Obama made clear his support for the Respect for Marriage Act, which would force federal government to recognise same-sex marriage
Latinos (67%)	• Although they are drawn to the traditional moral values espoused by the Republican Party because of their largely Catholic beliefs (and were effectively targeted by George W. Bush in this way), Latinos tend to be loyal as a minority group to the Democrats and are particularly attracted by their less hostile views on immigration • The Democrats have looked to offer some illegal immigrants a path to citizenship, in order to court the Latino vote • In contrast to the above, Republican-controlled states, including Arizona and Alabama, have introduced strict immigration laws, fuelling fears of racial profiling among the Latino community
Women (56%)	• Support is strongest among single young women who particularly favour the party's more pro-choice stance on abortion • NARAL Pro-Choice America has been deeply critical of what it deems as the Republican House's 'war on women', with attempts to restrict women's right to choose
African Americans (95%)	• Historically this group has been the party's most loyal constituency, with the numbers voting Democrat rarely falling below 90% • The Democrats' position on upholding civil rights and more interventionist approach to government, with much greater support for affirmative action, maintains this support

Examiner tip

For short-answer questions, such as those on why groups tend to vote for a particular party, it is best to develop three or four points fully in separate and distinct paragraphs. Avoid trying to cram in too many points, which would leave little time to explain each one. Make sure each point is supported by a relevant example.

Minor parties

For most commentators the USA is a two-party system, in which third parties face a range of obstacles to success. On a national level, third-party success has been very limited, although they have had some impact on the political system. The reasons for their lack of success are manifold. In some ways this lack of success is a product of the fact that the factions within the major parties allow them to cover a broad range of support, leaving little room on the political spectrum for minor parties. Primaries have also made infiltration of the main parties easier than challenging them, as best highlighted by the rise of Tea Party Republican challengers in the 2010 midterms. However, there remains a range of other obstacles to minority party achievement.

Obstacles to success

First-past-the-post electoral system

The use of this winner-takes-all system, which is exacerbated by the Electoral College, makes it very hard for minor parties, which do not have both widespread national support and regional strength in depth, to succeed. In this way, George Wallace secured 45 Electoral College votes with 13% of the vote in 1965, targeting southern states, while in 1992 Ross Perot achieved no Electoral College votes despite polling nearly 19% of the national vote.

Ballot access rules

State ballot access laws can be particularly stringent, soaking up the time and resources of minor parties. States such as California require a petition signed by 10% of the votes cast in the previous gubernatorial election, which amounts to over 1 million signatures for 2012.

Limited funding

The provision of federal matching funds in presidential elections works against minor parties, which require at least 5% of the previous vote for partial funding and 25% for full funding. In addition to the fact that this sets the bar too high for third-party candidates, with only three having achieved this since it was introduced, it also means that candidates, such as Perot in 1992, do not actually receive funding in the election cycle where they have had success. Given the huge cost, and restrictions, for getting on the ballot, as well as the lack of federal funding, minor parties find themselves in a 'catch-22' situation. They find it hard to raise money from pressure groups and PACs because they are unlikely to win. In 2008, John McCain, the only major-party candidate to accept federal funding, received $84 million from this source alone, while Ralph Nader, the most successful minor-party candidate, raised only $4 million in total.

Co-optation

The major parties in the USA, through co-optation, often act as 'sponge parties', absorbing the successful policies of minor-party candidates, thus nullifying their electoral success. In this way, Perot's commitment to financial policies which would

Two-party system A system in which two major parties secure the vast majority of the vote during public elections and thus dominate nearly every elected post. These parties will thus control the legislature and executive between them.

Knowledge check 10

What is the Electoral College?

Co-optation The process by which major parties adopt the successful policies of minor parties in order to neutralise their opposition.

balance the federal budget was rapidly absorbed by both Clinton and congressional Republicans.

Lack of media coverage

Given the obstacles mentioned above, minor-party candidates find it hard to secure any print or TV news coverage. In addition, they are usually excluded from the national presidential debates, as Nader was in 2000. Only Ross Perot in 1992 and John Anderson in 1980 have appeared in a presidential debate.

Impact of minor parties

Despite the lack of success in gaining electoral representation, many minor parties have still had an indirect impact on the US political system. This has been achieved on the one hand through influencing the political agenda and pushing certain issues towards the forefront of elections. An example is Ross Perot's success in 1992, which forced the major parties to focus on the issue of the budget deficit. Although he achieved no Electoral College votes that year, his policies were adopted by both Democratic President Bill Clinton and the Republican Congress, which achieved victory in 1994 with its commitment to a balanced budget as part of the Contract with America. As a result, the USA had a budget surplus by the end of Clinton's presidency.

Minor parties have also on occasion had an indirect impact on the eventual outcome of the election. This was most obviously the case in the 2000 presidential election, which swung on the result in Florida. Here Nader, who polled nearly 100,000 votes, arguably cost Al Gore the election when Bush achieved victory in the state by a margin of only 537 votes, meaning he ultimately won the Electoral College by just five votes, despite losing the overall popular vote.

Examiner tip

Be careful not to get drawn into detailing the impact or successes of minor parties in short-answer questions which *only* ask for factors which limit the success of minor parties.

Knowledge summary

- Appreciation of the ideological transformation of the two major parties from the broad non-ideological coalitions of the 1950s and 1960s into the more ideologically cohesive parties of today.

- Understanding of the extent of partisan politics in the USA, through evaluation of how far the two main parties are different from one another, and consideration of the influence of different factions within each party.

- Recognition of different groups of voters who typically support the two main parties, and the historical and contemporary reasons for this support.

- Awareness of debate around the extent to which parties remain relevant within the current political system, and how far they have come to be replaced by other bodies such as pressure groups; knowledge of the arguments for party renewal or party decline.

- Knowledge and understanding of the factors which limit the success of minor parties, as well as the impact they have had on the US political system.

Pressure groups

The role and influence of pressure groups is at the very heart of discussion and debate about the democratic nature of the US political system. Despite the Founding Fathers' distrust of 'factions', the intricate system of checks and balances and separation of powers meant that they in fact created a system open to external influence — one that enables and positively encourages the formation of pressure groups. The constitution created a number of access points, at both state and federal levels, along with a political system that encouraged political participation and an active citizenry, in order to better hold politicians to account. As a result, America today has a wide range of pressure groups, each actively involved in the political process and attempting to influence government in order to shape policy outcomes in its own interests.

The first aspect of this topic is therefore concerned with the *methods used by different pressure groups to attempt to influence the system,* and how far they are successful in achieving their aims. The range of access points has generated debate about the relative success of different pressure groups and their ability to influence public policy at federal and state levels. To some commentators, the sheer size or financial wealth of certain pressure groups gives them a distinct advantage over other smaller and less affluent groups. Similarly, there is the issue of the prominence of different pressure groups, in which some are able to achieve a disproportionate influence over the political system due to their insider status.

Linked to this is the second question of *whether pressure group activity is healthy to US democracy,* or whether it undermines the democratic values of electoral accountability and 'one person, one vote'. There is a view, embraced by many liberals in particular, that money has come to dominate the US political process. This view that the US system is one in which 'you've got to pay to play', and where wealthy individuals and groups can manipulate the political system to their own advantage, is a powerful one. The rising cost of US elections, with the 2008 and 2010 elections each costing more than $5 billion, has led many more liberally-minded political commentators to argue that the system benefits the rich at the expense of the poor. In contrast to this, in a nation which constitutionally enshrines 'freedom of speech' and encourages political participation, pressure group activity can be seen as fundamental to the values of the USA. Indeed, for many conservative commentators, pressure group activity should be left unconstrained by excessive federal regulation, while individuals should be free to engage in the political process without restrictions from federal government. They would argue that pressure group activity is beneficial for democracy and that it encourages a healthy competition between different groups, and actually prevents the accumulation of too much power in the hands of a few. Therefore, another key feature of this topic is to understand *the contemporary debate between those who believe pressure groups create an **elitist** power structure in the USA and those who believe they are fundamentally good for democracy* in creating a pluralist system of participation and compromise.

Knowledge check 11

Explain the US system of checks and balances and separation of powers.

Access points The openings in the political system which pressure groups use to try to advance their aims. In the USA there is a range of such openings available to pressure groups, within the executive, legislature and judiciary, at both federal and state levels.

Pluralist The idea that political power is shared among a broad range of groups which scrutinise each other and compete for influence. In this unit it refers to the idea that pressure groups hold government to account between elections, encourage political participation, and ensure all views in society are represented.

Range of pressure groups

The USA has a huge number of pressure groups, which represent a variety of issues and interests. There are a number of reasons to account for the existence of such a plethora of groups. The main reasons are listed below.

Access points

There are a large number of access points open to pressure groups in the US political system. The federalist nature of the US system enables groups to advance their interests to the executive and legislature at both state and federal levels. Alternatively, they can challenge decisions in the courts, organise the introduction of direct ballot initiatives or try to influence the outcome of pre-election primaries.

Expanding federal government

With an expansion in the size of federal government and the degree of regulatory control over businesses, a number of groups have sprung up to advance the interests of businesses, consumers and workers alike, in order to try and shape the policy framework to their advantage. Accordingly the **US Chamber of Commerce** represents the interests of its 300,000 businesses and trade groups, such as Texaco and Goldman Sachs, while the **AFL-CIO** combines 55 trade union groups, representing over 12 million workers in the USA.

Increasing partisanship

Arguably the ever more adversarial character of US politics, in which conservative and liberal groups compete for influence, has contributed to the growth of ideological and issue-based pressure groups. There has been a growth in the number of partisan think tanks such as the conservative **Heritage Foundation**, which is committed to 'limited government', or the **Centre for American Progress**, which in contrast is committed to 'progressive ideas'.

Similarly, the ideological divisions over a range of social issues have led to the creation of divergent pressure groups. Thus while **NARAL Pro-choice America** champions a woman's right to abortion, the **National Right to Life Committee** works against measures which allow abortions.

The growth of the **Tea Party** movement, which arose out of conservative grassroots discontent in 2009, also triggered the creation of its more liberal **Coffee Party** equivalent by January 2010.

Scrutiny

Growing distrust of government has led to the growth of public interest groups designed to improve political scrutiny, as well as issue-centred groups looking to inform the electorate about the voting records and policy positions of politicians. In this way, the **Centre for Responsive Politics** tracks the influence of money and lobbying activities on elections and public policy making. Likewise the **League of Conservation Voters** publishes a biennial 'Dirty Dozen' report of those politicians with the worst environmental track record.

Examiner tip

Examiners will not expect, or welcome, long-winded explanations of the different types of pressure groups in the USA. The best answers will be able to demonstrate a wider knowledge of pressure group activity in the USA which does not rely solely on examples from those groups which are popular among all candidates, such as the NRA or NAACP.

Methods and strategies

The huge number of access points open to US pressure groups means that they have a range of strategies available to them. The tactics used by individual pressure groups, however, will depend on a number of factors, such as their size, the funds at their disposal and which access points are open to them at any point in time. Thus those which are larger or better funded will be able to use a greater spread of tactics to target all three branches of the federal and state government. In contrast, other groups which cannot gain insider status will be forced to adopt more direct action outside the political system, such as mass protesting and public relations stunts, to gain publicity and media coverage. Nevertheless, there are a number of main strategies open to US pressure groups to enable them to influence state and federal lawmakers and/or executives.

Electioneering

Given the vast number and frequency of US elections, pressure groups are presented with a range of opportunities to take part in the electoral process, in an attempt to affect the outcome or shift the policy positions of candidates. Perhaps the two key areas in this respect are through the provision of funding to candidates, either directly or indirectly, and through endorsements and 'get-out-the-vote' activities.

Funding

Much of the electioneering in the USA is paid for by countless pressure and advocacy groups, which include:

- political action committees (PACs)
- 527s
- Super PACs

These groups all seek to influence how voters look at the candidates, and thus indirectly shape opinions about a political candidate or party, without necessarily mentioning a specific candidate or instructing people how to vote.

The significant growth of these funding vehicles, responsible for collecting and allocating money on behalf of a range of individuals and pressure groups who share common interests, has arisen following the introduction of electoral funding laws. They have become a means through which pressure groups can maximise their funding power. Alternatively, with later developments such as 527s, they have arisen from exploiting loopholes in the funding regulations system; this has allowed them to circumvent the restrictions, following successful legal challenges about the constitutionality of such funding regulations.

Political action committees (PACs)

Following the **Federal Election Campaign Act 1974** (FECA), which limited campaign donations to candidates, the number of political action committees (PACs) mushroomed, as they offered a way around this legislation. Although the maximum contribution to a PAC was $5,000, donations could be made to an unlimited

Political action committee An umbrella organisation which collects money from many lobby groups, and individuals, who are all concerned with the same issue. It uses these funds to support the campaign finances of sympathetic politicians and other advocacy groups.

number of PACs. The Federal Election Commission recorded that by 2008 there were over 4,238 PACs registered in the USA.

The rise of these PACs has contributed to the growth of electoral expenditure and arguably given greater influence to pressure groups that are able to pool donations and support. Although it is hard to evaluate the degree of influence that is exerted from these campaign contributions, there have been some notable examples to suggest they go some way to influence the decisions of lawmakers.

- In passing the 2008 **Telecom Amnesty**, given to telecoms groups helping with government wiretapping, Democrats who shifted support in favour of the amnesty received almost twice as much money from telecom PACs as Democrats who opposed the idea. On average, those who changed their votes collected $8,359 from these PACs from January 2005 through March 2008, while those who did not change their opposition collected $4,987.
- In 2009 the pressure group **Mobilization for Healthcare for All** led a protest against Democratic Senator Joe Lieberman, whom they accused of trying to undermine attempts to secure a 'public option', or government-funded health insurance, in the healthcare bill. They claimed his stance was shaped by his acceptance of more than $1 million in campaign contributions from the medical insurance industry during his time in the Senate.

527s

Following the Bipartisan Campaign Reform Act (BCRA) in 2002, which effectively meant that PACs could no longer directly fund adverts which support or oppose a candidate, a number of 527 groups began to appear. These pressure groups circumvented the 2002 regulations by not using 'magic words' to expressly advocate a candidate's election or defeat. There are two main ways in which 527s spend their money:

- **Voter mobilisation efforts:** This means encouraging people to register to vote and to get out and vote. It may seem to be non-partisan, but the location and group focused on is usually very partisan. Thus in 2006 the liberal **Moveon.org** group used a 527 to channel efforts to secure voters in a number of key Democrat-voting districts by making over 7 million phone calls, in their 'Call for Change' effort.
- **Advertising:** This may appear to focus on an issue, but in reality it hails or criticises a candidate in all but name. The 527 group **Swift Boat Vets for Truth** ran a series of adverts in 2004 which openly questioned Democratic presidential candidate John Kerry's 'false 1971 testimony' about the Vietnam War. Reports at the time suggested that over half the funds generated came from just three prominent Republican donors.

Super PACs

The Supreme Court decision in *Citizens United* v *FEC*, in January 2010, and the *Speechnow.org* v *FEC* ruling by the US Appeals Court, in July 2010, both served to lift many spending and contribution limits. As a result there has been an explosion of Super PACs, which can raise unlimited amounts of money to influence elections. Although these PACs must publicly disclose their finances, and they cannot coordinate with candidates or parties, they are free to advocate directly for or against a candidate. Though the impact of this is again hard to judge, the statistics from the 2010 midterms are startling:

- More than one Super PAC a day was registering with the FEC.
- Super PACs spent more than $8 million in September 2010.
- Those favouring Republican candidates outspent Democratic supporters by more than three to one.
- More than half of the total spending came from **American Crossroads**, a pro-Republican group supported by Karl Rove, the former adviser to George W. Bush.

Endorsements

Pressure groups can also look to exert influence through the mobilisation of members and supporters to vote for a candidate. This is particularly effective where members are single-issue swing voters or are present in sufficient numbers in key battleground areas. Thus the **NRA Political Victory Fund**, which grades and endorses candidates based on their voting records, is seen as particularly influential, given the claims of some political commentators that its members live disproportionately in 15 key battleground states and 40 battleground US House districts, meaning candidates are afraid of upsetting this important voting bloc.

Lobbying

Lobbying is the process through which pressure groups seek to build relations with lawmakers to secure favourable policy outcomes and influence the legislative agenda. With 12,997 registered lobbyists in 2010 and with 'K Street corridor' becoming the centre for Washington-based lobbyist firms, it is clear that lobbying is now a 'persuasion industry' in its own right. Indeed, to date, the US Chamber of Commerce has spent over $755 million on lobbying activities and there have been some noteworthy examples regarding the impact of lobbyists on the recent Healthcare Act. These include the following:

- The Sunlight Foundation highlighted how 20% of the campaign funds for Max Baucus, chair of the Senate Finance Committee, was contributed by lobbyists linked to **PhARMA**, representing the wealthy pharmaceutical industry. Some argue that this influenced his decision to exclude from initial discussions about healthcare reform in 2009 those pressure groups demanding wider healthcare coverage.
- In 2009, according to a study by the Center for Public Integrity, more than 1,750 companies and organisations hired about 4,525 lobbyists, who spent around $3.3 billion in order to influence the healthcare issue. This translated as eight healthcare lobbyists for each member of Congress.

Grassroots activism

The growth of the Tea Party movement, since its birth on 15 April 2009, over criticism of President Obama's economic policies, healthcare plans and 'big government' initiatives, shows the power of grassroots movements. A well-timed demonstration, such as the 1963 March on Washington by various civil rights groups, can help put pressure on Congress, or push an issue onto the legislative agenda. However, it may also be seen as a sign of pressure group weakness, or as a last resort for groups which are unable to gain insider status.

> **Examiner tip**
> Many of the examples of pressure group strategies to target the executive and lawmakers could equally be used to provide evidence that pressure groups are damaging to democracy. Certainly many of the examples of pressure group funding and lobbying activities could be used to support the argument that the system is fundamentally elitist and dominated by money.

> **Grassroots activism**
> Activities undertaken by ordinary members of pressure groups, which are seen to be free of party political control. The main forms of activity are marches and demonstrations aimed at raising awareness of issues among voters and politicians.

Ballot initiatives

Pressure groups unable to shape the picture at a federal level, or wishing to target state governments, can use the federalist nature of the USA to achieve their aims. With 24 states currently allowing **initiatives** and **propositions**, which put proposed laws onto the ballot at election time, pressure groups are provided with a powerful way to influence the political system through direct democracy. Thus pressure groups can exert influence through using their membership and resources to:

- **introduce ballot initiatives** — gathering the signatures needed, and promoting the measure, to get it placed on the ballot
- **coordinate a campaign** — establishing campaign offices and funding full-time staff, such as public relations firms
- **fund a campaign** — running advertising campaigns and producing promotional material
- **staff a campaign** — providing grassroots support and volunteers to generate support or opposition to an initiative

There have been some prominent examples in recent years of pressure group success in this area, most notably over the issue of same-sex marriages and affirmative action. Examples include the following:

- In 2008 **Proposition 8** was passed in California, which banned same-sex marriage. This saw over $82 million spent by various pressure groups, although interestingly those opposing the ban spent $4 million more than their opponents. There were also questions raised about the Utah-based Mormon church flooding the state with around 80–90% of the early volunteers and, according to Protect Marriage, contributing nearly half of the $39 million they raised.
- In 2009 **Stand For Marriage Maine** oversaw the successful collection of 100,000 signatures, which was nearly twice that required to get '**Question 1**', rejecting the same-sex marriage law in the state, onto the ballot. It also hired the California public relations firm, Schubert Flint, which ran the successful Proposition 8 campaign. In the end the measure succeeded with nearly 53% of votes.

However, it is worth noting that in 2010 all six of the ballot measures in Colorado failed and that in 2010 **Arizona 202**, the 'Stop Illegal Hiring' proposition, failed despite support from business interests which saw them spend 20 times more than opponents.

Knowledge check 14

What methods can pressure groups use to exert influence through initiatives and propositions?

Influence on the federal government

This aspect of the course looks at why each of the three federal branches of government offers different opportunities for pressure groups to advance their interests and thereby influence the political process. As well as the broad range of methods and strategies (outlined above) which are open to pressure groups in targeting members of the executive and legislature, there are a number of reasons why pressure groups might choose to target a specific branch of the government in order to achieve their aims.

Legislature

As the chief lawmaking body in the USA, Congress is an obvious target for pressure group activity. Attempts to build relations with members of Congress, through electioneering and lobbying, are part of the staple diet of many pressure groups. Indeed, securing the passage of legislation is a powerful way for pressure groups to gain influence over the political process. This is helped by the fact that the political system provides numerous access points and opportunities for pressure groups to influence the course of legislation through Congress. Of particular significance are the following:

- **Bicameral legislature:** Through both chambers, the House of Representatives and the Senate, groups have a broader range of possibilities to influence and shape legislation as it passes through either chamber.
- **Divided government:** The two chambers of Congress are often held by different parties, as was the case after the 2010 midterms, giving a pressure group a greater chance of at least watering down legislation it disapproves of.
- **Committee system:** The power of congressional committees, as the 'gatekeepers' to legislation, provides opportunities for pressure groups to shape or block legislation before it arrives on the floor of Congress.

There are also reasons why pressure groups might choose to focus their efforts on one of the chambers.

House of Representatives

As the House was given the exclusive power to initiate money bills, this makes it a significant target for groups wishing to secure a slice of the colossal annual federal budget, or those wishing to influence where that money is spent. In this way, the results of the 2010 midterms, in which the Republican Party gained control of the House, led to widespread demands from the Tea Party and other conservative pressure groups to defund the 2010 Healthcare Act, or what they dubbed 'ObamaCare'. Certainly the tense budget negotiations in January 2011, which saw the threat of a government shutdown, did lead to a deal which saw the pro-abortion group **Planned Parenthood** have its federal funding removed in the subsequent budget compromise deal.

Senate

The exclusive powers of the Senate make it a similar target for other pressure groups, especially given its powers in the following three areas.

Foreign policy

With the constitutional power to ratify treaties, which requires two-thirds of Senate support, the Senate is a target for many groups wishing to influence America's foreign policy position. Many commentators have pointed towards the power and insider status gained by the **American Israel Public Affairs Committee** (AIPAC). Indeed, in their 2007 book, two leading political scientists from the University of Chicago and Harvard claimed the Israel lobby had an almost unchallenged hold on Congress, being the most powerful interest group 'tirelessly working to move US foreign policy in Israel's direction'. Its importance is highlighted by the fact that at AIPAC's 2008

Examiner tip

As the course does not require an in-depth understanding of local and state-based politics, questions in this topic tend to focus on national access points. Therefore it is important to know how, and why, pressure groups use different methods for each branch of government and also to have relevant examples to judge the degree of success they enjoy.

LEARNING ZONE
COLEG CAMBRIA D....

Knowledge check 15

Name two reasons why pressure groups might seek to influence the US Senate.

annual convention the presidential candidates for both the main parties, McCain and Obama, addressed the gathering, as did the respective legislative leaders from both the Senate and the House.

Confirming appointments

The Senate is also responsible for confirming, by a simple majority, presidential appointments to many positions in the executive branch and, more importantly, to all posts in the federal judiciary. In recent times, the process of Supreme Court nominations has become increasingly politicised. Some argue it is dominated by pressure group activity, especially since the controversial rejection of Robert Bork, President Reagan's nominee in 1987, who was subjected to a series of attacks from liberal interest groups such as the **National Organization for Women** (NOW) and the **National Abortion Rights League**.

Filibuster A senator's right to unlimited debate, unless 60 senators vote to bring debate to a close. This gives individual or groups of senators the power to delay or prevent a vote on a bill they disagree with.

Filibuster

The Senate's unlimited right to debate is also a factor in many pressure groups' decisions to target individual senators, who can exert real power with the mere threat of a filibuster. In 2008 the **Climate Security Act**, which aimed to reduce greenhouse gas emissions, was successfully filibustered by a group of Republican senators following a concerted lobbying effort by oil and energy lobbyists, such as Exxon Mobil and the American Petroleum Institute, who argued it would damage the US economy.

Executive

As with the legislature, pressure groups in the USA are presented with two main options when looking to influence the executive. They can choose to target the president and his team of advisers directly, using many of the tactics outlined above. Alternatively, they can look to influence the federal bureaucracy, especially if they find the president is less receptive to their views.

Examiner tip

Good answers to questions about the influence of pressure group activity on the executive will mention both the direct impact on the president as well as the indirect influence on the federal bureaucracy. Thus you should look to include a review of the influence of lobbying, electioneering, endorsements and grassroots activities, as well as the impact of iron triangles and regulatory capture.

President

Although the system of checks and balances severely restricts the degree of presidential power, the president still holds a considerable amount of power, especially in setting the national legislative agenda. The president's position in moulding the legislative direction of the USA, through the annual State of the Union address and his powers of persuasion, can be used by pressure groups to achieve their aims. Similarly, pressure groups can encourage the president to use his executive orders to change the direction of policy, such as with the constant reinstatement and reversal of the 'Mexico City Policy', which bans federal funding for family planning clinics that give abortion advice. George W. Bush satisfied pro-life groups by reinstating the policy in 2001. However, one of Obama's earliest actions on assuming office was to reverse the policy to ensure federal funding went to these groups.

Federal bureaucracy

For those groups not ideologically supported by the president, there is still the opportunity to target and build relations with the relevant executive departments and regulatory bodies. Civil servants may well have long-term agendas which do not fit with the president's immediate priorities, allowing pressure groups access to try and shape policy and thwart the president's will. When this relationship involves the relevant congressional committee, an **iron triangle** (see below under 'Controversies and criticisms') can develop, which holds a firm grip on policy that presidents find hard to break. Similarly, pressure groups will look to develop relations with the relevant regulatory body which is supposed to be scrutinising them. When this develops into too cosy a relationship, there can be **regulatory capture** (see below), in which the 'watchdog' becomes the 'lapdog', as the pressure group exerts influence over the regulatory body charged with regulating it.

Judiciary

There has been much criticism of the Supreme Court's power of judicial review, with some commentators describing the justices as 'politicians in robes' due to the fact that many of their constitutional rulings are in effect judicial lawmaking. For this reason, and whether the criticisms are warranted or not, groups in the USA are uniquely positioned to influence judicial decisions in two main ways:

- **Litigation:** Funding test cases to the Supreme Court is a way in which pressure groups can secure a ruling which is favourable to their interests. The **National Rifle Association** (NRA) has in the past used the courts to challenge gun restriction laws across the USA, to uphold the constitutional 'right to bear arms'. In particular, its support of the *DC* v *Heller* case in 2008, and the *McDonald* v *Chicago* case in 2010, was important in securing the ruling that the 2nd Amendment covered an 'individual's right to possess a firearm'.
- **Amicus curiae:** By presenting legal briefings to a court which is undertaking judicial review, a pressure group would hope to sway the court's decision in its favour. These briefings have increased by over 800% since the 1940s, with over 100 being filed in the *Bollinger* cases, by pressure groups such as the **National Association for the Advancement of Colored People** (NAACP).

In addition, as mentioned above, pressure groups look to mould the overall makeup of the Supreme Court by influencing a president's choice of nominee or the Senate ratification process. A recent example of this was the withdrawal of George W. Bush's nominee Harriet Miers in 2005, which was seen as the product of a concerted campaign by conservative pressure groups, such as Christian Rights groups, which were worried about her position on a series of social issues.

Power of pressure groups

Overview

This topic looks at the debate surrounding the power and influence of pressure groups, and how far their activities and actions are damaging to US democracy. On the one hand, pluralists would argue that they are a sign of a healthy democracy through encouraging participation, scrutiny and engagement in the political process. However, others point towards their elitist nature, which allows a few, usually wealthy, pressure groups to dominate the system.

Amicus curiae The right of individuals or groups to present information to the court, in order to help them make their decision before a ruling is made. The term refers to a legal briefing which summarises a pressure group's standpoint on the legal issue being considered.

Examiner tip
Always check the focus of pressure group questions. Too often students are quick to reproduce a pre-planned essay on the elitist and pluralist arguments without specifically relating their points to the question set. This is especially the case when students are asked about the influence of pressure groups over issues, or the polarising effects of pressure group activity.

Positive view of pressure group activity

The first key argument is that pressure groups provide a healthy 'free market' of opinion, and give empowerment to all US citizens, who are able to use them as vehicles for influencing their political leaders. Many conservatives would point to the array of access points, which give multiple opportunities for everyone to be heard and make a contribution to shaping society.

There is strong evidence that the actions of pressure groups have in the past protected minority groups, who might be expected to be excluded from an elitist system. The role of black civil rights groups, such as the NAACP, in securing legislative equality with the passage of the Voting Rights and the Civil Rights Acts, along with their influence in dismantling the southern system of segregation, through *Brown* v *Board of Education*, are two cases in point. Similarly, in 2003, the *Lawrence* v *Texas* ruling, which was funded by **Lambda Legal** (an advocacy group for lesbian and gays), declared laws which discriminated against gays unconstitutional.

Limitations and constraints

Other commentators would further point out that the system works to limit existing barriers which stop full participation. In their view, the system of regulations and constraints placed on pressure groups prevents them from becoming too powerful, or dominating the system. In particular, they would point towards the following examples:

- **Federal Election Campaigns Act 1974:** restricted the influence of wealth by setting limits for individual donations and establishing a system of federal funding for major party candidates.
- **Bipartisan Campaign Reform Act 2002:** tightened the restrictions from the previous act by regulating soft money and introducing advertising restrictions.
- **Lobbying Disclosure Act 1995:** widened the requirements for lobbyists to register their activities while also banning the giving of gifts.
- **Honest Leadership and Open Government Act 2007:** attempted to close the revolving door by introducing a 'cooling-off' period after leaving office, while also extending the ban on gifts and requirements for full disclosure of lobbying activities.

Negative view of pressure group activity

Examiner tip
The criticisms of pressure group activity can be grouped into five main areas, although there is significant overlap between them. You might refer to the earlier points regarding the dominance of money in the political system through pressure group funding and lobbying activities, as well as the points which follow regarding the insider status gained by certain groups.

The alternative view is that America is dominated by a power elite, and that efforts to try and constrain the power of pressure groups, to ensure there is a level playing field in which all groups have the same opportunities, have failed. Thus, for certain political commentators, the wide range of access points can be exploited only by those groups with the resources and wealth to take advantage of them. In this way, certain pressure groups have come to dominate, using their greater numbers or wealth to monopolise the political system. As a result, commentators contend that smaller groups are unable to exert any real political power as they do not have the wealth, voting power or insider connections to secure the ear of those in power. Evidence for this argument can be found in the influence of funding and lobbying on the political system, as well as in the existence of three main areas of controversy in the USA:

- revolving-door syndrome
- iron triangles
- regulatory capture

Controversies and criticisms

Revolving-door syndrome

A high proportion of lobbyists have come from the ranks of former politicians, or staff members. This leads to the accusation that US politics is dominated by an insider elite, whose members are able to influence the political system through the 'revolving door', which gives them constant access to those in power.

Furthermore, critics also point out that this creates situations where politicians are unduly influenced, in creating public policy, by the lucrative prospect of a high-paid job for a lobbying firm when they leave politics. There are many example of this overlap between those in politics and lobbying:

- **John Ashcroft**, who served 6 years in the Senate and 4 years as the US Attorney General, set up the Ashcroft Group, upon leaving office. In 2005, less than a month after collecting $220,000 from Oracle Corporation, John Ashcroft used his contacts to secure a multibillion-dollar acquisition contract for Oracle with the Department of Justice.
- The Livingston Group, a lobbying consultancy, was set up by the former Republican Speaker for the House, **Bob Livingstone**.
- **Darleen Druyun**, a Pentagon official responsible for overseeing the purchase of military equipment, secured jobs at Boeing for her daughter and son-in-law just months after awarding them a $23.5-billion contract. Two years later in 2002 she herself took up a lucrative job at Boeing, with a salary of a quarter of a million dollars.

Iron triangle

An iron triangle is a political community featuring three very powerful players in the political process. When pressure groups, congressional committees and the federal bureaucracy have shared aims, they can develop a very strong relationship. This gives them an iron grip on public policy, enabling them to effectively dictate and block attempts by Congress or the president for reform. Perhaps the most criticised iron triangle has been the **military industrial complex** (MIC), the strong relationship between the Defense Department, the congressional armed forces committees and the leading weapons manufacturers, which some argue has contributed to the USA's huge defence budgets. The following case serves as an example:

- In 2010 the $726-billion **Defense Authorization Bill** highlighted the issue of iron triangles. US Defense Secretary Robert Gates unsuccessfully urged President Barack Obama to veto the bill, which contained funding for unwanted projects. For years Gates had been trying to battle defence contractors, such as those providing C-17 transport planes, in order to cut the budget; but the defence committees were keen to protect jobs in key states, and the Pentagon was keen to maintain a high degree of defence expenditure. Gates ultimately had only limited success in trying to achieve financial reform at the Pentagon, and in reining in some expensive contracts, due to the combined efforts of the Pentagon, defence contractors and influential defence committee members to retain them.

Revolving-door syndrome The idea that the same people dominate public policy making. As many lobbyists are former politicians, or their aides, the view stands that the same people remain in the political world to control policy.

Knowledge check 16

What is lobbying?

Iron triangle A strong relationship between a pressure group, the relevant congressional committee and the relevant government department or agency in an attempt to guarantee the policy outcomes to the benefit of all three groups.

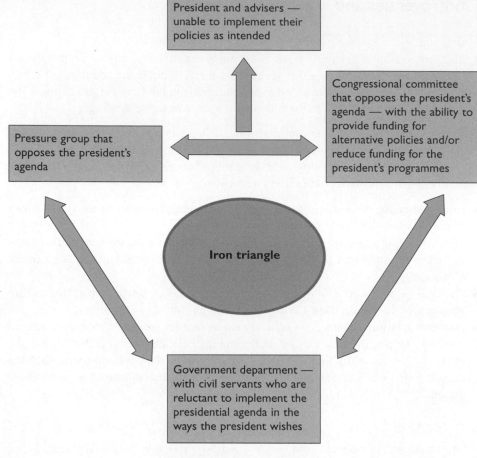

Figure 1 The iron triangle

Regulatory capture

A close relationship between regulatory agencies and the pressure groups that they are supposed to be overseeing can mean that government watchdog agencies often turn into lapdogs. This has been a recent criticism laid at the door of the financial and energy regulatory bodies, in the wake of the recent banking crisis and the Gulf of Mexico oil disaster. This is evidenced by the following:

- A **Securities and Exchange Commission report** in March 2008 pointed towards its own failures in regulating the financial sector with a system which allowed banks to 'opt in or out of supervision voluntarily'. Many blamed the heavy lobbying from all five big investment banks in 2004 for this voluntary system.
- The 2010 **Interior Department review** into the Gulf of Mexico oil disaster found that it resulted from the failed regulation of those who were supposed to be policing the nation's offshore drilling facilities.

- Knowledge and analysis of the issue of pressure group influence and how far such groups act as democratic vehicles for participation and scrutiny or merely serve to further entrench the position of a wealthy, influential minority.

- Understanding of the range of access points available to US pressure groups, and evaluation of how far this creates an open system in which all are able to engage in the political process, or how far this allows large, wealthy groups to dominate.

- Understanding of the range of methods available to pressure groups in influencing the different branches of federal government, as well as ability to judge the success with which pressure groups are able to advance their agendas.

- Awareness and appreciation of the debate around the extent to which pressure groups' power is a good thing, including the elitist and pluralist arguments based around the extent to which money and insider connections allow certain groups to dominate the system.

- A solid understanding of the various regulations placed upon pressure group activity and contemporary criticisms of their actions.

Racial and ethnic politics

The 1776 US Declaration of Independence declared that 'all men are created equal'. This was a fundamental principle upon which the Founding Fathers based the US political system. Part of this topic surrounds the contemporary American debate about the extent to which the history of racial discrimination, and lack of opportunities for significant racial and ethnic minorities, means that *equality for all has been, and remains today, a distant dream for significant numbers of African Americans and Latinos.*

The history of publicly-sanctioned discrimination, which effectively removed the civil rights of many racial minorities, has led many to question whether the USA is a genuinely meritocratic society. For many liberal commentators, the product of this history of racial discrimination is the continuing existence of institutional racism and lack of opportunities for racial and ethnic minorities. They would point towards the fact that these minorities remain at an inherent disadvantage with regard to their lack of economic progress and educational attainment. Conservative commentators, in contrast, argue that the USA has rid itself of racism and is today a **post-racial society**, in which there is a true equality of opportunity for all. They point towards the growing political success of minorities, particularly the election of Barack Obama as the first African-American president in US history, as well as the increasing affluence of many minorities, including the emergence of a substantial black middle class.

The second aspect of this topic is the political debate surrounding *the strategies to remedy these past historical injustices.* As can be expected, many conservatives do not feel there is any justification for, and fundamentally disagree with, any attempt by the government to introduce measures to rectify these historical issues of discrimination. They cite the progress made by minorities as evidence that the USA is now a land of opportunity for all, while they also distrust any programmes which extend government interference into the everyday lives of individuals. For

Institutional racism
The idea that racism is embedded in many US organisations. It may not be overt racism, but it leads to the indirect disadvantage of minorities through selection or promotion procedures which perpetuate racial and ethnic stereotypes. Thus, for example, many minorities are seen to struggle to achieve university places compared to their white peers.

You need to understand the divide between liberal and conservative opinion about whether the USA is truly equal and how far racism still persists. For maximum marks, aim to provide a balanced answer which includes specific evidence of equality and minority successes as well as evidence of inequality and the ongoing barriers which racial and ethnic minorities face.

With essay questions for this topic, avoid long descriptions and narratives about the history of racism in the USA. Remember it is not a history essay; you must answer the question set by the examiner and relate points to the political debate in America today.

many liberals, however, this ignores the responsibility of the American government to remedy the problems. Liberals point towards the political and moral responsibility of the US government to redress the continuing barriers to educational and economic achievement facing minorities.

A final aspect of this topic is to consider the *current debate surrounding immigration reform*, which has increasingly come to the forefront of contemporary politics with the growing importance of the Latino vote in US elections. In particular, students will need to be aware of the *reasons for this debate and the alternative reforms suggested*.

History of inequality

Despite the intentions of the Founding Fathers to create a political system which would protect and uphold the core values of individual liberty and equality of opportunity, the history of the USA is one in which the constitution enshrined slavery and excluded Native Americans from the rights given to the white, Anglo-Saxon, Protestant Americans (WASPs).

Constitutional protection of slavery

Although the US Constitution does not explicitly uphold slavery, it did implicitly authorise it. Indeed, constitutionally, slaves — who did not retain voting rights themselves — were originally counted as three-fifths of a person in the apportionment of seats to the House of Representatives and Electoral College; this resulted in the southern slave-owning states being significantly over-represented. In addition, the 1857 *Dred Scott* v *Sandford* ruling by the Supreme Court ruled that slavery was not only constitutionally permissible but could not be limited to the southern states.

Abolition of slavery

Although the American Civil War, and the 13th Amendment, banned slavery, this did not lead to the end of racial discrimination for African Americans, particularly in the former slave-owning states. Here black people saw the erosion of their right to vote, and a system of state laws were passed, known collectively as **Jim Crow laws**, which enforced segregation and in effect made black people second-class citizens. Again this was given constitutional protection by the Supreme Court, which ruled in favour of 'separate but equal' facilities in the 1896 *Plessy* v *Ferguson* case.

The southern states continued to deprive African Americans of their basic civil rights by establishing a system which disadvantaged black people politically, socially and economically. Their voting rights were restricted by complex registration laws, which were sometimes based in literacy or comprehension tests. They had to use separate, inferior facilities, such as washrooms and water fountains. Furthermore, their position was perpetuated by a segregated public education system, in which African-American schools received significantly less funding. Even those blacks who moved north did not always find their position improved. Many still faced informal segregation and life in black ghettoes, while racist employment practices, in which some were barred from certain professions or were the first to be fired when economic conditions changed, persisted.

Civil rights

A series of civil rights movements, protesting against racist laws, swept across America from the 1950s onwards. Two key events acted as a catalyst for these protests: the *Brown* v *Board of Education* Supreme Court decision and the Montgomery bus boycott. The 1954 Supreme Court verdict, which overturned *Plessy* and declared the practice of school segregation unconstitutional on the grounds that it was 'inherently unequal', acted as a spur to civil rights campaigners. Similarly, the challenge to segregation on Alabama's bus network, which began with the arrest of Rosa Parks, a black women who refused to vacate her seat for a white man in 1954, had wide-reaching consequences and gave birth to the Civil Rights movement.

The passage of the Civil Rights Act 1964 and the Voting Rights Act 1965 marked the end of these protests. The acts served to abolish the state-based practice of formal and informal discrimination by enforcing equality upon all states and terminating the practice of indirectly disenfranchising black people.

However, questions still remain about how far this marked an end to discrimination for African Americans in particular and minorities in general. This question of ongoing discrimination also lies at the heart of the current debate about how far America has, and whether it should even look to have, erased this history of racial discrimination and 'inherited guilt'. This feeds into the contemporary debate about the extent to which the USA is now an equal country, in which every race and ethnicity can succeed.

Knowledge check 17

What is the full name of the pressure group which funded the *Brown* v *Board of Education* case in 1954?

Examiner tip

Always check questions to see whether they refer to issues of equality and opportunities facing *all* ethnic and racial minorities, including Latinos, or whether they refer only to African Americans. Remember you will get no reward for knowledge and analysis which does not focus on the question.

Continuing inequalities

Many liberals point towards the continuing existence of inequalities in the political, social and economic life chances of minorities to suggest that minorities, especially those from Latino and African-American communities, are at a fundamental disadvantage in modern America. For them, the fact that many minorities remain under-represented at nearly every level of government, that there are more than twice as many blacks and Latinos living below the poverty line than whites, as well as the vast differences in educational attainment between ethnic and racial groups, are evidence of these ongoing inequalities.

Evidence of political inequalities

The lack of political representation for minority groups can be seen as evidence that there exists a fundamental difference between the dream of equality of opportunity and the political reality that exists in America today. There is a strong argument among many liberals that the barriers to minority political achievement demonstrate the failings of the American political system, which favours the wealthy white establishment at the expense of minorities. The following can be cited in support of this argument:

- Despite black people accounting for 13% and Latinos for 12% of the US population, in the 112th Congress their share of the seats in the House was only 9.6% for African Americans (42 members) and 6.6% for Latinos (29 members).

- There is only one Native American in Congress — Illinois Representative Tom Cole.
- Only six African Americans and seven Latinos have ever served in the US Senate.
- Much of the minority political representation in America is secured as a result of preferential redistricting and the creation of majority-minority districts, such as Illinois 4th's Latino 'earmuff district', rather than race-less voting.

Evidence of social problems

The life chances of many minority groups are seen to be severely limited, which would further suggest that minorities are at an inherent disadvantage compared to whites. It can be argued that the existence of institutional racism in the USA, especially within the education and criminal justice systems, continues to impact upon minorities today. Bill Clinton referred to the 'cancer' of disparities in sentencing, such as the existence of mandatory minimums for first-time cocaine use where 1 gram of crack cocaine, which is more common among minority communities, was equated with 100 grams of powder cocaine predominantly associated with white Americans. Further examples of this enduring lack of social opportunity can be seen in the following:

- Jonathan Kozol's 2005 book, *The Shame of the Nation*, refers to America's 'apartheid' schools by arguing that a system of segregation still exists in America, with largely black urban schools in which students lack the educational opportunities offered to those in more affluent areas.
- Two reports in 2010, released by the Education Trust, found that while 60% of whites graduated from university within 6 years of starting their course, this was the case for only 49% of Latinos and 40% of African Americans.
- David R. Roediger, professor at the University of Illinois, referred to the 'highly racialised anti-crime political appeals' that caused a sevenfold increase in incarceration rates between 1975 and 2005. This has particularly affected minorities: in 2008, 60% of the prison population were people of colour, with African Americans seven times and Latinos three times more likely to be imprisoned than white men.
- The 2006 book *Locked Out* highlights the problems of disenfranchisement in the USA, where 13 states have removed the right to vote, for life, for felony convictions. As a result, in several American states one in four black men cannot vote and nationally it is estimated that 13% of blacks have lost the right to vote.
- The passage of **Arizona SB1070** in 2010, which requires Latinos to register for and carry state identification, shows the continuance of state-sanctioned profiling. Much as the idea of 'driving while black' showed the injustices of racial profiling, this is seen as evidence of the existence of racial and ethnic stereotyping in America, which undermines claims of equality.

Evidence of economic disparities

In economic terms there still exists a huge variance in the positions of African Americans and Latinos when compared to whites. This is seen as a barrier to minority opportunity, and key economic data, including the following, highlights the prevailing problems.

- Recent unemployment rates stood at 15.8% for blacks, 12.4% for Latinos, but just 8.8% for whites.

- A 2010 study by Brandeis University found that whites were five times wealthier than blacks, with white families' assets worth $100,000 compared to just $5,000 for African Americans.
- In 2008 the research group United for a Fair Economy, in its annual State of the Dream report, estimated that an equalisation of black and white household wealth would not occur for a further 500 years.
- The above report, titled 'Foreclosure', also highlighted how minorities, who were three times more likely to have subprime loans, were significantly hit by the subprime mortgage crisis and stood to lose as much as $200 billion of wealth.
- A 2011 report, issued by the Alliance for Board Diversity, found that the share of Fortune 100 board seats held by black men dropped from just 7.8% in 2004 to a mere 4.2% by 2011.
- The same report found that there was not a single Latino female board chair of a Fortune 500 company in 2010.

Post-racial America

In an article in the *New Republic* in 2000, entitled 'Race Over', black Harvard professor Orlando Paterson claimed that race is no longer an issue in America, given the dramatic gains made by African Americans since the 1970s. In addition to those who argue that racial and ethnic minorities have made considerable progress, other, largely conservative, individuals point to the successes of other minority groups in the USA, which they refer to as 'model minorities'.

Evidence of political success

There is significant evidence of minority political representation across America, which gives weight to the view that America has extinguished the legacy of slavery and discrimination to become a truly colour-blind society.

- As well as Obama's successful bid for the presidency, there are a number of leading minority politicians such as long-term Congressman John Conyers, freshman Senator Marco Rubio and the Attorney General Eric Holder.
- Presidential appointments have also given the Supreme Court a greater degree of racial and ethnic balance, with justices such as the African American Clarence Thomas and Latino Sonia Sotomayor.
- At a state level, minorities have also made good progress. In 2009 Colorado, despite having only a 4% black population, became the first state in which both the state legislative leaders were African American. Similarly, in the Deep South state of Mississippi, where 37% of the population is black, African Americans hold 29% of the seats on the state legislature.

Evidence of social advancement

In their 2003 book *No Excuses*, Stephan and Abigail Thernstrom argued that educational attainment is based largely on ethnic cultural factors. They refer to the positive work ethic of model minorities such as Asian Americans, when compared to the Latino and African-American communities, as a reason for varying achievement levels, rather than any lack of social or educational opportunities.

Model minority A minority ethnic or racial group which achieves a greater degree of success when compared to other groups. The term is usually used to identify the higher achievement of one ethnic minority group over another.

LEARNING ZONE
COLEG CAMBRIA DEESIDE

Further evidence of minority social advancement can be seen in the following:

- The numbers of African Americans completing high school rose from 72% in 1972 to 86% in 2005. For Latinos there was a similar rise from 56% to 70%.
- In a 2007 article for the *New York Times*, Orlando Paterson argued that the disparity in black imprisonment rates may not be solely down to judicial bias or racism but to the high rate of violent crime within the community — the rate at which blacks commit homicides being seven times higher than whites.
- A number of states have introduced policies to advance racial diversity in education. For example, the Texan Ten Percent Plan guarantees students who graduate in the top 10% of their high school class automatic admission to all state-funded universities.

Evidence of economic achievement

Despite variances in the degree of economic achievement, many conservatives argue that the existence of an increasingly affluent black middle class, as well as the success of many other minority groups, is evidence that there are no longer any barriers to economic achievement.

- In 2009, 46.2% of blacks and 48.4% of Latinos owned their own home.
- By 2000 the proportion of African Americans in white-collar jobs had risen to 74.5%.
- A 2011 report from Packaged Facts predicted that the buying power of African Americans would hit $1.1 trillion by 2012.
- The same report stated that the USA has 2.4 million affluent African-American households with incomes of $75,000 or above.
- Census data shows that in 2004 average earnings among Asian men was as high as $46,888, while the figure for black men stood at $32,686.
- By 2002 over half (52%) of all black married-couple families had incomes of at least $50,000.

Affirmative action

Affirmative action generally means giving preferential treatment to minorities in admissions to universities or employment opportunities for government and private businesses. More specifically, it refers to a range of policies originally developed to correct decades of discrimination and to give disadvantaged minorities a boost. Some say that the diversity of American society today, as opposed to that of 50 years ago, indicates that the programmes have been a success. In contrast, others, particularly conservatives, think the policies were never, or are no longer, needed and that they lead to more problems than they solve.

History of affirmative action

Formal equality for African Americans was gained through the Civil Rights Act 1964 and the Voting Rights Act 1965. Since then some Americans have argued that this established a clear and legal framework for **equality of opportunity**, in that all races were now free from legal discrimination and were able to succeed. Particularly

Knowledge check 18

What is meant by a post-racial America?

Examiner tip

Ensure that you are clear on the attitudes of different groups towards affirmative action and also that you are able to evaluate its impact. For the exam you should understand all the arguments about whether the policies remain, or ever were, necessary, and be able to judge the extent of their success.

those with conservative views argued that this gave legal protection to all races, ensuring de facto equality.

However, the focus soon shifted away from formal and legal equality towards more substantive equality. Many liberals argued that there was a need for **equality of outcome** to level the playing field for previously disadvantaged groups. For many, there was now a need for America to address the fact that African Americans in particular were at a historical disadvantage, as they lagged behind whites in terms of income, employment and educational attainment. What use, they argued, was the right to attend the best schools and apply for the best jobs if blacks did not have the qualifications and money to make it a reality?

To those who supported substantive equality (including President Johnson), the 1964 and 1965 Acts were the beginnings, not the end, of a campaign for equality. A series of policies were adopted that became known as **affirmative action.** The measures established ranged from 'soft' measures to target job adverts at minorities to 'hard' measures which included giving quotas and preferences to these groups. In this way, the Equal Employment Opportunity Commission was set up under President Kennedy, with the executive order to use affirmative action in federally-funded projects. This was extended under Nixon's Philadelphia Plan, which gave preference to construction companies who actively hired ethnic minorities, thus giving a boost to employment opportunities for African Americans in the construction industry.

Restrictions to affirmative action

Affirmative action came under immediate scrutiny from those who were critical of what they deemed to be positive discrimination and an increase in federal government intervention. From the 1970s onwards the policies of affirmative action were opposed by those politicians and commentators who saw it as merely reverse discrimination, pointing towards the unconstitutional basis for advantaging one group at the expense of another.

In addition, since 1978, a series of Supreme Court decisions have gone some way to water down and limit the forms of affirmative action deemed constitutional, without explicitly declaring affirmative action to be unconstitutional. The most notable of these rulings are listed below.

- *Regents of the University of California* **v** *Bakke* **(1978**) accepted that race could be one factor, among many, in university admissions but could not directly disadvantage majority applicants.
- *United Steelworkers* **v** *Weber* **(1979)** upheld the decision to establish a 50% quota of employees from ethnic minorities as it would not lead to job losses from white workers.
- *Adarand Constructors* **v** *Pena* **(1995)** did not declare affirmative action unconstitutional but re-established the need for 'strict scrutiny' to ensure that federal affirmative action programmes had a specific purpose and justification. In this case, the ruling struck down the Department of Transportation's preference system in issuing road-building contracts as too general and not 'narrowly tailored' to specifically target discriminated groups.

Knowledge check 19

How do the views of conservatives and liberals differ over the issue of affirmative action?

Knowledge check 20

Explain two key ways in which affirmative action has been restricted since its introduction in the 1960s.

- *Gratz* v *Bollinger* **(2003)** declared the University of Michigan's racial quota system of admissions unconstitutional as it was 'too mechanistic' in awarding all minorities 20 of the 150 points needed for admission.
- *Grutter* v *Bollinger* **(2003)** ruled that University of Michigan's Law School admissions programme was constitutional as it used an 'individualised' affirmative action programme, in which race was only a 'plus factor'. Although it upheld as constitutional the continued use of certain affirmative action programmes, it did suggest that this may only be necessary for a further 25 years.

As can be seen, affirmative action has been, and remains, a contentious issue. There is a range of opinion about whether it is necessary and the key question remains largely unanswered – should affirmative action be used to end discrimination or is it discriminatory itself?

In a series of initiatives and propositions in recent years the issue of affirmative action's place in the USA has become further clouded. By 2010 at least five states had seen the successful introduction of measures to ban affirmative action.

- **California Proposition 209 (1996)** banned affirmative action by stating the state could not 'discriminate against, or grant preferential treatment…on the basis of race'.
- **Michigan Proposal 2 (2006)**, a state-wide initiative which banned the use of affirmative action in public employment, education or contracting.
- **Arizona Proposition 107 (2010)** banned, by a vote of over 60%, the consideration of race, ethnicity or gender by the state government, including in public college and university admissions.

Arguments against affirmative action

- **Reverse discrimination:** Conservatives believe that the broad nature of affirmative action programmes, even without quotas, can lead to rich minorities being given preference over poor white applicants.
- **Lower standards and motivation:** A 2010 report, by the Education trust, pointed out that within six years of enrolling for a degree, the graduation rates for white students stood at 60% while it was only 49% for Latinos and 40% for African Americans. Similarly in his 2004 article for the Stanford Law Review the UCLA's Richard Sander's concluded that 'preferences themselves put (black students) at an enormous academic disadvantage.'
- **Prevents a truly colour-blind society:** Some, like Supreme Court Justice Clarence Thomas, argue affirmative action is condescending and insulting; in fact he stated 'Any effort, policy or program that in some way accepts the notion that Blacks are inferior is a non-starter with me.'
- **Undermines minority achievement:** Too often, minority achievements are demeaned by affirmative action. Indeed Michael Savage, the conservative radio host, claimed that Barack Obama, in the month before his election, 'benefited from affirmative action, stepping over more qualified white men'.

Arguments in favour of affirmative action

- **Promotes diversity:** The need to achieve a fully integrated and diverse range of university applicants was indeed a factor in the 2003 *Grutter* v *Bollinger* case when justices expressed the need for a diverse student body.

Reverse discrimination
The idea that race-based affirmative action is racist in itself by actively disadvantaging white people. This is seen to be linked to the critical view of many Americans when using the terms 'positive discrimination' and 'racial preferences' for affirmative action programmes.

Knowledge check 21

What were the two Supreme Court rulings in 2003, regarding affirmative action, and what did they decide?

- **Levels the playing field:** In his book of 2004, *The Hidden Cost of Being African American*, Thomas Shapiro points towards the continuing disadvantage facing minority students. The widespread disparity in income, poverty and unemployment between white and black students shows that they start out at a disadvantage in their college or job application process. It is therefore argued that affirmative action is still necessary to have a positive impact on this situation. Indeed it was highlighted by Bowen and Bock, in their book *The Shape of the River*, how race-based university admission practices can successfully advance the life chances of minority students.
- **Breaks down racial stereotypes:** The opportunities gained, directly or indirectly, through affirmative action have given minorities the chance to show they are every bit as capable as whites in a range of fields.
- **Compensation:** In the words of President Johnson, at Howard University in 1960, 'You do not wipe away the scars of centuries by saying: Now you are free to go where you want, do as you desire, choose the leaders you please.'

Individual and group views on affirmative action

- **Colin Powell, former Republican Secretary of State**, in 2003 described himself as a 'strong proponent' of affirmative action as the Supreme Court was ruling on the Bollinger cases.
- **Nancy Pelosi, former Democrat House Speaker**, was given a 100% rating on affirmative action, in 2006, by the NAACP and said in 2003, 'Affirmative action in education gives students a ladder to climb over the barriers to opportunity.'
- **Barack Obama**, said in 2009 that although 'crude quotas' were unconstitutional, he still supported, in certain circumstances, 'taking into account issues of past discrimination' and the role of affirmative action in ensuring the 'diversity of a workforce or a student body'.
- **Rand Paul, Republican Senator for Kentucky**, supports repeal of all measures and suggested in 2010 that private businesses should be free to choose employees without any restrictions, even if this could be deemed discriminatory.

> **Examiner tip**
>
> All students should look to have a solid understanding of the different views among critics and proponents of affirmative action. However, the best answers will also present the opinions of specific individuals, who may well have more moderate or conservative views of affirmative action.

Alternatives to affirmative action

Abolition

- There has recently been a strong push among American states to ban racial or gender preferences. Much of this has been a reaction to the controversial and unprecedented decisions in the Bollinger cases, sponsored by the conservative pressure group the Centre for Individual Rights. These cases effectively declared 'mechanistic' racial quotas unconstitutional, without specifically declaring affirmative action unconstitutional. In particular, the *Grutter* v *Bollinger* case, by a slender 5–4 majority, upheld affirmative action but stated that admissions must be flexible, and reaffirmed that they could not be crude **quotas**, because race must be considered as one among many other admission criteria.
- Many conservative groups, such as the Center for Equal Opportunity, call for a complete ban on all forms of affirmative action and have led attempts to legally challenge affirmative action.
- In 2010, nearly 60% of Arizona voters supported Proposition 107, joining Michigan, California, Florida, Texas and Washington in banning the use of race or sex in admissions considerations.

> **Quota** A specific number or percentage of educational or work placements set aside for minority groups. Where the setting of quotas is too broad and 'mechanistic', a range of Supreme Court judgements have declared this unconstitutional.

In this way the Florida governor, Jeb Bush, decided in 1999 to abolish affirmative action in university admissions and state contracting, with his 'One Florida' initiative. Although this led to widespread demonstrations, conservatives would counter criticisms with the fact that over the decade from 1999 to 2009, total state enrolment among Latinos rose from 13.8% to 18%, while black enrolment remained relatively static at 13.6%.

Class- and income-based action

- Some opponents argue that affirmative action benefits middle- and upper-class minorities at the expense of lower-class Caucasians. Thus some argue that there is a need for class-based, or income-based, affirmative action which does not consider race or ethnicity.
- A *New York Times* poll showed, in 2005, that almost 85% of Americans favoured preferences based on socioeconomic, rather than racial, status. Furthermore, in states such as California, which have banned affirmative action, the introduction of a class-based system has been an important means of continuing affirmative action programmes which assist minority groups.
- However, the African American Policy Forum believes that the class-based argument is wrongly based on the idea that more affluent minorities do not experience racial and gender-based discrimination. It believes that: 'Race-conscious affirmative action remains necessary to address race-based obstacles.'

School and cultural reform

- A number of largely conservative individuals argue that the inability of minorities to compete is because those minorities need to be 'Americanised' and encouraged to conform more closely to the mainstream cultural norms of the USA.
- In Texas a system was set up in 1998, whereby the top 10% of all students at each school qualify for a Texas State University of their choice. This ensures that minority students are not competing with students from schools that are better funded and resourced.

Reparations

- Since 1989 Congressman John Conyers Jnr from Michigan has introduced a bill every year to study the case for **reparations**. He urges the federal government to undertake a thorough review which will lead to financial compensation to the descendants of African slavery.
- Though calls for reparations do not hold widespread appeal in America, the 'Millions for Reparations' march, in 2002, did see over 50,000 people descend on Washington DC.

Immigration

Immigration is becoming a critical issue, and also deeply divisive, given the growing importance of the Latino vote in many states along the Mexican border. On the one hand, conservatives see it as strictly an issue of controlling immigration and securing US borders from illegal immigrants. However, liberals claim that immigrants are

Examiner tip

With questions that require an evaluation of alternative methods to ensure racial and ethnic equality in the USA, wherever possible refer to specific individuals or groups or provide examples of specific programmes which are available in the USA today.

Reparations
Compensation paid to individuals who have suffered from previous state-sponsored discrimination. In the USA there is debate about whether this should be in the form of a financial payment, made to the descendants of those who suffered, or through the provision of healthcare coverage.

people with rights who are essential to a failing economy, and therefore should be encouraged to integrate with US society through a nationwide amnesty programme.

Given that there are an estimated 11.2 million, mostly Latino, illegal immigrants in the USA, there is a bitter divide over how best to tackle the situation. This is especially the case given the changing demographics in the USA, with the Mexican-American population growing over the last decade by 11.4 million. Their political impact has been pointed out by the Pew Hispanic Center, which noted that the Latino vote in 2010 reached 6.9% of all voters — a significant voting bloc given their concentration in many border and western states. This is also evidenced by the surging Latino population in Texas (37.6% in 2010), which Democrats have targeted for victory in the forthcoming Senate race, with retired general Ricardo Sanchez looking to secure the Democrat candidacy for 2012.

Immigration reform

Amnesty

Some groups including the **National Council of La Raza**, the largest Latino pressure group in the USA, have called for a path to citizenship for the existing 12 million undocumented immigrants in the USA. This was the basis of a 2001 bipartisan **DREAM Act**, which would have given citizenship to those who had graduated high school and university or undertaken 2 years' military service. However, the bill which was passed by the House in December 2010 failed to overcome a filibuster led by Republican Senator Jeff Sessions, who argued that the bill amounted to a reward for lawbreaking.

The entrenched views on this issue were highlighted by the comments of Republican Representative Elton Galley, following an Obama speech on the issue of immigration, that 'providing a path to citizenship for illegal immigrants...is amnesty. Amnesty will not pass Congress, Mr President.'

Border control

The issue of immigration has taken a new turn in recent years. Some argue for a focus on policing the borders, while conservatives call for tighter immigration laws which would require local law-enforcement officials to question those they suspect of breaking the law. With the passage of immigration laws in states such as Arizona, Georgia and Alabama, the Obama administration has looked to challenge this state-based legislation, arguing that the laws are unconstitutional because immigration is a federal matter beyond state jurisdiction. Although such laws were thus put on hold by federal courts, they remain contentious issues, with the distinct possibility of a Supreme Court ruling on the matter.

The partisan nature of this debate is highlighted by fact that no action has been taken by the Obama administration against sanctuary cities that refuse to cooperate with the federal government on immigration matters. Indeed a spokeswoman for Attorney General Eric Holder said there was a difference between 'not enforcing federal law, as so-called sanctuary cities have done, and a state passing its own immigration policy that actively interferes with federal law'.

Examiner tip
As this is a contemporary issue, you are advised to stay up to date on the latest news regarding immigration. A particularly good website is the *Washington Post* site 'The Battle Over Immigration'.

Amnesty A general pardon granted by a government, which would allow illegal immigrants to apply to become American citizens.

Sanctuary city A term given to a city which protects illegal immigrants. This is usually through the process of not enforcing federal immigration laws, by preventing police or municipal employees from inquiring about immigration status.

The increasing significance of this issue is highlighted by the fact that some have called immigration 'the new slavery', in the way that it has come to divide America. Thus the 2012 election will in part be fought by those liberals who feel immigration is a national issue, and support the path to citizenship for illegal immigrants, and those conservatives who fear 'big government', and invoke the rights of states in deciding their own approach to dealing with immigration.

Knowledge summary

- An appreciation of the extent to which race is deeply ingrained in the history and political values of the USA with its focus on fairness.
- A detailed evaluation of how far contemporary America can be viewed as a fundamentally equal society in which everyone, regardless of race or ethnicity, has the same opportunities to succeed.
- Understanding of the divide between those conservatives who believe that there are no longer any barriers to opportunity and those liberals who point towards the enduring legacy of discrimination which acts as an obstacle to minority success.
- Awareness of the continuing debate over the extent to which overt or institutional racism persists in the USA and the degree to which the problems faced by minorities are a result of personal and cultural factors which should be addressed within their own communities.
- Awareness of the controversy over the degree to which government should intervene to help minority groups, largely though affirmative action.
- Knowledge and understanding of the range of alternative strategies proposed to ensure equality of opportunity for all racial and ethnic groups.
- Understanding of why immigration reform has become such a controversial political topic in the USA and knowledge of the range of suggested strategies in dealing with immigration.

Questions & Answers

How to use this section

At the beginning of this section there is an explanation of the assessment objectives and a guide as to how the marks for each assessment objective are distributed among the different questions on the paper. There follow some specimen examination questions. These are neither past examination questions, nor future examination questions, but they are very similar to the kind of questions you will face.

The best way to use this section of the guide is to look at each question and make notes on how you would go about answering it, including the key facts and knowledge you would use, relevant examples, the analysis, arguments and evaluations you would deploy and the conclusions you would reach. You should also make a plan of how you would answer the whole question, taking into account the examiner tip (indicated by the icon ⓔ) immediately below the question.

After each specimen question there are two exemplar answers. One will be a strong answer and the other will be either weak or of medium quality. The strength of each specimen answer is indicated in the examiner commentary (again indicated by the icon ⓔ) that follows it. In the commentary there are also notes on the answer's strengths and weaknesses and an indication as to how marks would be awarded for each assessment objective. Now compare these specimen answers with your own notes. Amend your notes to bring them to the standard of the stronger specimen. Having done all this, you can now attempt a full answer to the question, aiming to avoid the weaknesses and include the strengths that have been indicated in the specimen answers and explanations of the marks.

Of course you may use the information in your own way. The above guidance is merely a recommendation. Remember, however, that simply 'learning' the strong specimen answers will not help — these are answers to specimen questions, not to the questions you will actually face. It is preferable to learn how to answer questions 'actively', that is by writing your own answers, using the questions and answers as a guide. In this way you will be able to tackle effectively any questions that may come your way in the examination.

Assessment objectives overview

	AO1 Knowledge and understanding	AO2 Analysis and evaluation	Synopticity	AO3 Coherent argument	Total
Short answer	5 marks	7 marks		3 marks	**15 marks**
Essay question	12 marks	12 marks	12 marks	9 marks	**45 marks**

Knowledge and understanding

Assessment objective 1 involves the breadth and depth of a student's knowledge, which must be relevant to the question being asked. Look to show knowledge of the key terms in a question through definitions and the correct use of political terminology.

In this way questions about criticisms of the presidential nomination process, for example, will need to show knowledge of frontloading, invisible primary, raiding, voter apathy etc.

Analysis and evaluation

Assessment objective 2 is concerned with the quality of your explanation and evaluation of the question set. In answering questions, stronger students will look to present a rounded argument which evaluates a range of factors and weigh up the value of individual factors.

In this way a question on the extent to which the Republican Party is dominated by conservatives, for example, will look to present a balanced argument. There will, however, be a clear judgement on the question and the basis for that judgement will be apparent.

Synoptic debate

Synoptic marks are *only awarded for essay questions*. They are awarded for considering at least two sides of an argument, although some questions will have a broader range of viewpoints. The obvious way to safeguard synoptic marks is to ensure you do not present an essay which is wholly or largely one-sided. You must look to show a very well-defined sense of opposing arguments.

In this way questions which ask, for example, how far race-based affirmative action has been a success and is still needed will require, as a minimum, viewpoints that it has *and* has not succeeded. However, more developed responses will consider the range of views among liberals that affirmative action must continue, be adapted or be replaced with more far reaching policies such as reparations, as well as the views of conservatives that affirmative action was never required in the first place or is no longer necessary.

Developing an argument

To meet the requirements of assessment objective 3, essay questions in particular will require the presentation of a range of views on an issue. However, in presenting and analysing these views your own line of argument must be indicated at the start, and be clear throughout. To produce a good coherent argument you must look to:

- **signpost your judgement** and the basis for it at the start
- **support your argument** by presenting the key factors which sustain your argument, using detailed and relevant examples as evidence to back up each point
- **unravel counter-arguments** by explaining the weaknesses of other viewpoints

This is not simply presenting a list of points for or against and summing up at the end. Examiners are looking for a sustained attempt to present and unpick different arguments on an issue.

In this way questions about the extent to which pressure groups weaken democracy, for example, will require an explanation of viewpoints that they do and do not weaken democracy. However, stronger answers will look to weigh up these views, in order to present a cohesive argument about whether they are positive or negative to the US democratic process.

Short-answer guidance

Timing is key for these questions as you are only given 15 minutes to respond. Thus these answers require you to immediately address the question, avoiding long-winded and descriptive introductions.

Also, ensure you read the question. There are no synoptic marks for short answers, so questions *do not* require a balanced response *unless* the question specifically asks you to address both sides or signals that you should with words such as 'to what extent' or 'how far' etc.

These answers are best addressed by focusing on fully developing three to four factors, in separate paragraphs, which answer the question set.

Essay guidance

You should look to spend 45 minutes on each essay question, but ensure you spend at least 5 of those minutes planning your response. The danger is that students jump into questions, having selected a topic, without understanding the requirements of a specific question.

You should also make sure you refer back to the question *throughout* your essay, so your answer does not drift away from it and lack coherence.

If you struggle with structuring your answer, make sure you get the basics right:

- Start with an introduction which sets out the debate and signposts your argument.
- Present three to four well-developed arguments for each side of the question, showing evaluation of each argument presented.
- Conclude with a summary of the question and clear judgement on the strongest argument and basis for its strength.

Question 1 **Elections and voting**

Assess the importance of National Party Conventions. (15 marks)

Ⓔ Most short-answer questions have a narrow focus and will only ask you, for example, to consider the 'strengths' or 'advantages' of an aspect of the political system. With these questions it is important not to stray into discussions of 'weaknesses' or 'disadvantages'. However, the word 'assess' in this question points towards the need for an evaluation of the significance of National Party Conventions, to consider the extent to which they have become meaningless and serve no purpose. Students are thus expected to provide evidence that they are both significant and insignificant.

Student A

Originally National Party Conventions, before the existence of primaries, were used to choose the party candidate for the presidential race **a**. However, the use of primaries in particular has led to the decrease in importance of party conventions.

Ⓔ This is a solid start to the question. It is well focused on the issue of importance and **a** provides a clear and early judgement, which also signposts the evidential basis for this, namely the rise of primaries.

Although the Convention officially chooses the party's candidate for the presidential race, since the use of primaries and especially since a process of frontloading, most obviously seen by the 2008 Tsunami Tuesday, delegates often know who the candidate is due to be in advance **b**. This is because other candidates drop out early on in the primary race, as candidates need an absolute majority to win. Thus in 2008, with over 4,000 Democratic delegates attending, Obama needed more than 2,000 delegate votes to secure victory **c**. However, despite this being the closest race in memory, Hillary Clinton still conceded the race 4 days after the last primary, and nearly 3 months before the Denver Convention. Thus it is clear that the National Convention merely rubberstamps the result of the primary race, and has very little significance **d**.

Ⓔ Also a very focused paragraph, **b** this clearly establishes the line of argument from the outset that the formal and traditional role of the convention, in choosing a presidential candidate, has ended. More importantly, the student has identified what they view as the main reason for this change, specifically primaries and frontloading. The student goes on to **c** develop a detailed and relevant example of this from 2008, while **d** reinforcing their analytical judgement that conventions no longer serve a useful purpose.

Similarly its role of defining the party platform **e** and generating serious debate about the direction the party should take has taken second place to just presenting a positive face to the media. As has the job of selecting the vice-presidential running mate **f**, which is also often known well in advance, and decided by the primary winner, rather than the party. With the party platforms being so vague it is clear that conventions serve very little practical purpose.

e The student continues to develop their argument by pointing towards two other factors which they judge have diminished the importance of conventions, that of **e** defining a party platform and **f** selecting the vice-presidential candidate. However, this answer could be further improved by supporting these points with relevant examples, such as the fact that Obama announced his choice of Joe Biden 2 days before, and McCain announced Palin as his choice 3 days before, the respective conventions opened in 2008.

> However, this is not to say they are insignificant as they do give an opportunity to create unity within the party after months of divisive campaigning. This is currently one of the most important and growing informal aspects of the National Convention as it is important to 'fire up' not only the party faithful but ordinary voters **g**. It is a moment where unity is important, as seen in both 2008 conventions when Clinton spoke of her support for Obama and when McCain chose Palin to help energise his conservative faithful **h**. Similarly, the media coverage and 'bounce' in the polls acts as a springboard into the election campaign. Certainly the success of the 2004 Republican Convention, held in New York after 9/11, led to a lead in the polls for the Republicans.

e Here the student shows that they are 'assessing' the question by clarifying the level of their judgement in recognising that conventions remain important in creating party unity. They specifically relate this to the informal functions of conventions in **g** enthusing the core party members, as well as **h** the political role of appealing and presenting a united front to the electorate.

> Despite this, it is clear that the formal roles of the conventions are no longer important and it now merely serves as a media circus with an attempt to present a positive face of the party **i**. It has sacrificed serious political debate and discussion for media coverage and false unity before the presidential election.

e This is a clear and concise conclusion, which clearly **i** reiterates the student's judgement on the question. It confirms the strength of the answer.

Overall this answer makes three well-developed points, which are all supported by relevant and detailed examples, about b the lack of a formal role in selecting the presidential candidate, and g the informal roles of enthusing the party faithful and h appealing to the electorate. It is also credited for mentioning the two points, albeit less well developed, about the insignificant role of conventions in e defining the party platform and f choosing the vice-presidential candidate. The clear level of structure, in which each point is well developed in separate paragraphs, and the fluency of the communication make it a very strong response, which would achieve a good A grade in the exam.

14/15 marks awarded.

Student B

National Party Conventions are held once every 4 years when there is a presidential election. It is a meeting of the main delegates of a party with the aim of choosing the candidate for the presidential campaign **a**. Both parties hold conventions following the results of the party primaries and their functions are to choose the presidential candidate, unite the party, develop a party platform and announce the vice-presidential candidate **b**.

🄔 This is a solid opening, which shows an understanding of **a** what National Conventions are and **b** the functions they fulfil. However, it is a very general and descriptive paragraph which does not fully signal the student's intention to 'assess' importance, instead focusing on what conventions do.

There is debate, however, as the increased use of primaries, since the 1970s, as opposed to caucuses, has been criticised as demeaning the importance of National Party Conventions **c**. The main reason for this is because the use of primaries means that the presidential nominee is often known well before the convention **d**, thus its main function is obsolete. However, as witnessed within the Democratic Party's primaries in 2008, the winner is not always clear. Barack Obama and Hillary Clinton fought a bitter battle up to the convention, where the superdelegates ultimately made the final decision **e**.

🄔 The second paragraph more clearly **c** links to the question of importance, by **d** pointing out the impact of primaries in reducing the formal role of selecting the presidential candidate. Although these points are well made, they lack a relevant example, and **e** the attempt to assess the question by weighing up the importance of the 2008 election is slightly flawed, given that Clinton conceded to Obama on 7 June, more than 2 months before the Democratic Convention.

On the other hand, the National Party Conventions provide an important role of uniting a party **f**. With infighting from the party throughout the primaries, rifts can occur and divide the party's core. Thus the Conventions boost morale behind the winning candidate by uniting the party through the discussion of party policies and gathering support from those who might be doubtful. The image of a united party is essential for winning the presidency. In 2008, for example, John McCain used the Republican convention to draw the party together and provide a focus with issues put aside after splits with other candidates **g**.

🄔 This shows a good attempt to assess and balance the student's response to the question **f** by looking at the conventions' role in securing party unity. It also rightly suggests that this is a result of the need to heal the wounds and rifts rising from the primary campaign. Again, however, it does not fully develop its evidence to support this argument, with **g** the example from 2008 lacking specific detail on how the party was drawn together, such as through the choice of Palin as the running mate, or the ways in which they were divided, perhaps by the success of Mike Huckabee in winning support among core conservative Republicans.

The choice of the vice-president is also not a role any longer of the convention as the president chooses this beforehand by trying to balance the ticket **h**. He chooses a candidate who complements his own weaknesses and this is announced well before the convention, such as with Obama and Biden. Therefore it is apparent that National Party Conventions remain important within the role of presidential nominations and, with the phenomenon of frontloading and primaries, their function to unite the party has grown in importance **i**.

e The conclusion is confused in its structure by **h** presenting another relevant point regarding the lack of importance in choosing the running mate, while **i** at the same time trying to summarise the student's judgement that conventions do play an important role in uniting the party.

With the lack of structure and development of points throughout, but given its solid knowledge and attempt to address the question, this answer would achieve a strong C grade in the exam. It does make three reasonably developed points, but they are not always well supported by relevant and detailed examples. Although the student shows a sound understanding of the question, they do not fully 'assess' the importance of conventions and the examples given are not always fully related to the point being made or sufficiently developed to achieve a higher mark.

9/15 marks awarded.

Question 2 **Political parties**

To what extent is the Democratic Party now progressively liberal? (15 marks)

ⓔ Although this is a short-answer question, because it states 'To what extent', it is clear that it is looking for a balanced evaluation of evidence that the Democrats are progressively liberal, against evidence that they are more moderate or conservative-minded. Students must focus specifically on the Democratic Party, rather than straying into references to the Republicans or the wider debate surrounding party renewal and decline theories. It is a question in which stronger answers will evaluate how far the Democrats are a cohesive and liberal body, or how far they are a fractious party made up of a range of individuals and factions competing for influence and which has become increasingly dominated by the more progressively liberal democrats.

Student A

For a party to conform to a liberal identity it must advocate traditionally liberal views such as increased public spending and a dove-like foreign policy **a**. To be socially liberal it would support policies such as pro-choice and restrictions on gun ownership. In this context the Democratic Party can be considered very liberal **b**. However, the conservative, Blue Dog, democrats within the party have been able to capitalise on the current divided government and press for much more conservative policies, such as the extension of the Bush tax cuts for a further 2 years in 2010 and the cuts to public spending seen in the most recent budget compromise **c**. So it is not appropriate at this time to call the Democratic Party liberal.

ⓔ Despite the vague start, in which the student **a** describes the general policy positions of liberals, this introduction does quickly **b** refer back to the question to outline the student's judgement. **c** Indeed this judgement is supported with a specific reference to contemporary events and the example given is relevant and detailed.

Despite this the Democratic Party in general can be viewed as largely liberal, as seen by its efforts to provide affordable healthcare, which was part of the liberal '6 for 06' campaign pledge in the 2006 midterms, led by Nancy Pelosi. This and the more recent repeal of the 'Don't ask, don't tell' policy, giving gays the right to openly serve in the US armed forces, shows that the party can rightly be seen as following a liberal ideology **d**.

ⓔ The student is quick to consider alternative evidence, with a good spread of examples to suggest the Democrats have in general adopted a series of more liberal policies, with reference to **d** affordable healthcare, '6 for 06' and 'Don't ask, don't tell'.

However, with Republicans taking control of the House, and following the surge in support for Tea Party Republicans, such as Rand Paul, it is clear that the Democrats have more recently been forced to curb their liberal streak in order to compromise with the more conservative views of the Republicans **e**. Indeed Obama compromised his own budget by extending Bush tax cuts, even to those earning over $200,000, and by removing the funding for family planning clinics which conduct abortions, such as Planned Parenthood. Similarly Obama has been more willing in the midst of an economic crisis to cut spending and follow a conservative programme of deep cuts to the public sector **f**.

e This paragraph shows that the student is assessing the 'extent' to which Democrats are liberal, in **e** making a clear argument that the Democrats have been forced to compromise their progressive liberalism and adopt a more conservative stance on a range of issues. Again this is **f** well supported with a range of contemporary examples.

This divided government, and the need for compromise in the face of a serious electoral defeat in the 2010 midterms, has forced the Democratic Party to abandon many of its more progressively liberal views **g**. Indeed the decision by Obama to continue to use the Guantanamo detention facility, despite early campaign commitments to close it, and the sanctioning of the US forces' attack in Pakistan, which led to Osama bin Laden's death, could all point towards a more conservative and 'hawkish' approach from the Democrats in the run-up to the 2012 elections **h**.

e Again the conclusion **g** sustains the argument that the Democratic Party has, for electoral reasons, deserted its progressively liberal position. It clearly **h** reinforces this argument with a developed evaluation of the shift in foreign policy approach to support the claim that the Democrats are more conservative-minded.

The strong focus on the question and use of a broad range of very recent, comprehensive and relevant examples would ensure this candidate achieves an A grade. Overall it is an excellent answer, presenting a balanced response, clearly addressing the question and evaluating a range of recent examples.

13/15 marks awarded.

Student B

The two-party system in the USA contains the Republican Party and the Democratic Party. The Democrats are traditionally more left wing than the Republicans and their policies reflect this. They support measures such as gay rights and affirmative action, which are opposed by the Republicans **a**. The reason for this was because of the break-up of the Solid South, when the Democrats supported the 1964 Civil Rights Act, and since then they have become the more liberal party **b**.

e The introduction is not very good, or particularly relevant to the question, as it merely gives **a** a general outline of the basic ideological viewpoints of both main parties and **b** the historical foundations of the liberal Democratic Party.

The main reason to suggest they are progressively liberal is Barack Obama's 2010 Healthcare Act **c**. This was a very liberal policy that came from the left-most people of the Democratic Party. It was favoured by liberals as it gives the poorest Americans healthcare coverage, even if it did not go as far as some wanted in getting the government involved in providing healthcare **d**.

(e) The second paragraph is much more relevant to the question and **c** begins to outline the argument that the Democrats are liberal. The answer does give an overview example of the 2010 Healthcare Act and implies some assessment by **d** referring to the limits of this measure. However, this example could be more fully developed, perhaps with reference to the removal of the 'public option' (i.e. the option for people to buy a federal government insurance plan).

> Another reason one could see the Democratic Party as progressively liberal is its views on abortion and gay marriage **e**. The majority of Democrats are pro-choice and in favour of gay marriage, and states such as California have legalised abortion and gay marriage **f**. As well as this the Democrats have made recent moves to let gays fight in the armed forces **g**.

(e) This is a confusing paragraph, which **e** asserts that the Democrats are all liberal given their stance on abortion and gay rights. **f** The first two examples would be given little credit by the examiner as they do not specifically relate to the Democrats. **g** The third example is more rewardable, although it is not a well-made point about the repeal of 'Don't ask, don't tell' in December 2010.

> However, there are also members of the party that do not follow suit. The southern Blue Dog Democrats, like Ben Nelson of Nebraska, are more like Republicans with moderate conservative views **h**. They were important in watering down the Healthcare Act with the Bart Stupak amendment, which secured the removal of federal funding for abortion clinics **i**.

(e) This is a much better paragraph, which points towards the existence of factions within the party by **h** specifically mentioning the conservative Blue Dogs and naming an individual within that faction. More importantly, the student **i** assesses their influence and provides detailed evidence of their ability to water down the Healthcare Act.

> In conclusion, the Democratic Party has shown since 2006 that it is progressively liberal, with Nancy Pelosi and Obama pushing forward liberal policies, despite opposition from conservative Democrats **j**. This is best seen by the attempts to spend money to get the economy going, while conservatives and the Tea Party Republicans want to cut money and spending.

(e) The conclusion does clearly **j** summarise the student's judgement, and provides a further relevant, if broad and unspecific, point to support this, namely the liberal spending policies when contrasted to the Tea Party Republicans.

Overall this is a solid response showing some sound understanding of the question, and would be strong enough to achieve a C grade in the exam. However, it could be much improved. It needs to be more focused on the question set, and to more fully develop the examples given or make them more relevant and specific to the points the student is trying to make.

9/15 marks awarded.

Question 3 **Pressure groups**

How far does pressure group activity in the USA advantage the wealthy while disadvantaging the poor?

(45 marks)

e Essay questions often begin with 'How far…' or 'To what extent…'. This is a signal that you must cover both sides of a question, i.e. how far it is and is not the case, while also having a clear judgement and line of argument throughout. In this instance the question asks you to analyse the importance of money in the US political system, and how far this gives more wealthy pressure groups a distinct advantage over those which are less wealthy.

Student A

There is considerable debate in the USA about the Democratic nature of pressure group activity, and the belief among many conservative-minded politicians that the plurality of pressure group activity creates a system where everyone has opportunities to participate, including minorities and the poor, in order to affect the political system and present their views to lawmakers. Though there is considerable evidence of this, such as the success of achieving the 1964 Civil Rights Act by the NAACP and other black civil rights groups, these successes are few and far between in a system which largely benefits the wealthy. Indeed many more liberally-minded commentators argue that the US system is dominated by money, and has created an elitist system where only the wealthy can succeed, and this has created a political system where, in the words of former Senator Ted Kennedy, it is 'the best Congress money can buy' **a**.

e This introduction has a clear focus on the question and effectively **a** sets out the synoptic debate on the question by outlining the pluralist and elitist arguments, with brief examples, while also signalling the judgement on the question.

Despite this it would be wrong to claim that all access points and every aspect of pressure group activity in the USA benefit only the wealthy, and certainly one of the key methods open to all pressure groups has been that of litigation, in seeking Supreme Court decisions which are favourable to a pressure group's aims **b**. There have been a number of high-profile examples of poorer and minority group interests being furthered in this way. Perhaps the obvious example is the *Brown* v *Board of Education* decision, which overturned the system of segregation in the USA, in particular benefiting the education of many poor black students. Similarly the 2003 *Lawrence* v *Texas* decision upheld, as constitutional, the rights of minority groups to engage in gay relations without facing legal prosecution **c**. Despite these examples, however, it is undeniable that well-funded pressure groups have also used judicial review to benefit their own agenda, which at times was at the expense of less wealthy pressure groups. In this way the NRA has launched a number of legal challenges to overturn restrictions on gun ownership, such as its success in overturning San Francisco's 2005 Proposition H and more recently its success in securing a Supreme Court decision on the 'right to bear arms' in *DC* v *Heller* **d**.

ⓔ The second paragraph then **b** sets out a key method of influence used by less well-funded pressure groups within the US political system. This is **c** well supported by two relevant examples of pressure group success in this area. However, the candidate is quick to **d** analyse the extent to which this is true and qualify their initial judgement by showing the success of more wealthy pressure groups in funding litigation cases in the USA.

In this way it is clear that the US political system does favour those with greater funding. Despite attempts to curtail the influence of pressure group money on political decisions, this has not curtailed the influence of money. Reforms such as the 1974 FECA, setting limits of $1,000 in 'hard money donations', or the 2002 BCRA, which effectively banned 'soft money' and limited-issue ads immediately prior to elections, have done little to limit the influence of money. US elections continue to see wealthy pressure groups using other avenues to channel money to politicians, through PACs and 527s **e**. The influence of the K-Street corridor has led some scholars, such as Stanford law professor Lawrence Lessig, to argue that money is effectively being used to buy political influence, in order for members of Congress to secure their tenure in office. Groups such as the Sunlight Foundation have cast light on this issue, highlighting for example how 20% of the campaign funds for Max Baucus, chairman of the Senate Finance Committee, was contributed by PhARMA and that this influenced his decision to exclude less wealthy pressure groups, demanding wider healthcare coverage, from initial discussions about healthcare reform in 2009. Similarly in passing the 2008 Telecoms amnesty, given to telecoms groups helping with government wiretapping, the Democrats who shifted support for the amnesty were shown to receive twice as much money, on average, from telecoms PACs than Democrats who opposed the idea **f**. In a system which has open access for lobbyists it is clear that money has brought influence for those pressure groups who can afford to 'pay to play'.

ⓔ The student continues a well-balanced approach, with a clear line of argument, in the third paragraph. The student **e** outlines the campaign reform acts, which go some way to encouraging an equal playing field for pressure groups, while analysing and developing their judgement on how wealthy pressure groups have managed to sidestep these laws to give themselves a greater degree of influence over the political process. Again the argument is **f** well supported with developed examples to show how the wealthy pressure groups have gained greater access at the expense of those who are less well funded.

Despite this there have been notable regulations imposed on the lobbying activities of wealthy pressure groups, to try to establish a level playing field for all groups, regardless of wealth. In this way the 1995 Lobbying Disclosure Act and the 2007 Honest Leadership and Open Government Act have gone some way to reduce the worst examples of money corruption by pressure groups, with bans on gifts and the widening of disclosure laws for all lobbyists **g**. Indeed the tide of opinion against wealthy pressure groups was best highlighted in 2008 when Obama referred to the negative impact, on policies, of 'lobbyists which crush them with their money and influence' and he refused campaign donations from registered lobbyists, instead generating finances from many small donors over his internet site.

e The line of argument is continued well in the two subsequent paragraphs, which begin by **g** clearly setting out the key regulations on lobbying activity and the ways in which these have more recently reduced the influence of money.

> However, it is undeniable that the effect of these laws, on limiting lobbying by wealthy pressure groups, has been limited. Indeed it has done little to restrict the influence of a power elite, through the 'revolving door' and establishment of iron triangles, by powerful and wealthy pressure groups. In this way the existence of the powerful defence lobby is shown by the problems former US Defense Secretary, Robert Gates, had in cutting defence spending, and is more recently seen in the 2010 Defense Authorization Bill which, according to CNN, exceeded $726 billion. These strong relations by wealthy business groups are best highlighted by the case of Darleen Druyun, a former acquisition official, responsible for awarding Boeing a $23.5 billion contract 2 years before she left her job at the Pentagon, in 2002, to take up a job at Boeing herself, with a salary of a quarter of a million dollars. Attempts to curtail this influence with a 2-year 'cooling-off' period will have little effect on an industry so dominated by money and political influence **h**.

e Here the argument is well qualified through **h** an evaluation of the continuing existence of the 'revolving-door syndrome' and of 'iron triangles', which the student uses to demonstrate that wealthy pressure groups benefit at the expense of the poor.

> In conclusion, it is clear that relatively poor pressure groups can impact on the political system either through the encouragement of participation, such as with the 'million mom' march, or in scrutinising government, as undertaken by the League of Conservation voters' 'Dirty Dozen', which highlights congressional members' poor voting record on environmental issues. However, America has a system largely dominated by wealthy pressure groups, who use their wealth to take advantage of the many access points, which is largely at the expense of smaller and less well-funded groups. Examples such as the defeat of McCain's Tobacco Bill in 1998 by a $40m lobbying effort, led by British American Tobacco, shows that ultimately money can enable pressure groups to thwart the popular will of the majority and that it creates a widespread disparity of influence among groups **i**.

e A well-balanced conclusion, which **i** reaffirms the student's judgement on the question. Overall this is a very strong answer which would achieve a high A grade in the exam.

AO1 KNOWLEDGE AND UNDERSTANDING: Throughout the answer the student uses an excellent and broad range of examples, all of which are relevant to the question set and very well developed. In this way **f** the example in the third paragraph, on campaign funds, mentions the group which brought this to light, the Sunlight Foundation, names the individual and his position, Max Baucus of the Senate Finance Committee, while also detailing the level of funding received from PhARMA, 20%, and how it seemed to sway Baucus' decisions, to exclude other groups from initial discussions on healthcare reform.

AO2 EVALUATION AND ANALYSIS: Throughout the essay there is a strong evaluative and analytical note, in which the student looks to develop a well-supported argument by showing how and why they are weighting their argument in favour of the question.

SYNOPTICITY: Though this essay has a clear line of argument, it does set this into an understanding of the wider debate, and provides evidence to support at least two views on the question.

AO3 COMMUNICATION: The essay flows very well, and while forwarding a strong argument in favour, has structured an answer which has clearly broken the question down to present both sides of the debate.

45/45 marks awarded: 12/12 for AO1, 12/12 for AO2, 12/12 for synopticity, 9/9 for AO3.

Student B

A pressure group is a body of people who seek to influence the political process, without standing for elections. There are a range of different types of pressure groups, but the main ones are membership groups, in which people join to suit their interests. Examples of this are the NRA, and sectional pressure groups like the trade union AFL-CIO or the CBI **a**. They also use many different types of pressure group activity because America has an open system and there are many access points, at both a federal and state level, which all mean pressure groups massively impact on the political system **b**.

ⓔ This introduction, though showing a degree of knowledge, is particularly weak because it **a** merely defines and sets out the different types of pressure groups. **b** Even the summary in the final sentence does not directly relate to the essay question, which requires more focus on the different levels of influence exerted by pressure groups based on their relative wealth.

In America, as some argue, all pressure groups are therefore powerful. However, it is true to say that some are more powerful than others **c**. As one politician said, 'money is the mother's milk of politics', and this is certainly true in America as wealthy pressure groups use the system to press their own interests, while poor groups are left behind. Certainly the fact that elections are getting more expensive, with the 2008 election the first to cost more than $1 billion, shows how wealthy pressure groups are increasingly using money to buy influence. More recently, the pharmaceutical and insurance industries have used their wealth to run adverts and support the campaigns of congressmen to affect the Healthcare Act. They were successful in restricting the coverage of the bill so that private firms and drugs companies will still make millions from the US healthcare system **d**.

ⓔ The second paragraph is **c** more directly related to the question, with a clear line of argument established at the beginning. Though much of the initial evidence to back up the view, that wealthy groups dominate the political process, is somewhat general, **d** there is a more rewardable example towards the end of the paragraph.

Wealthy pressure groups are also at an advantage in using the courts to defend their interests as they use this branch by funding cases, and getting decisions from the Supreme Court, which is a very costly approach **e**. The NRA, one of America's richest pressure groups, has launched a number of cases against states and federal government using its wealth to get the courts to uphold the 'right to bear arms'. The most recent one was **f** in Washington DC and the court declared that individuals do have this right, showing how money protects a pressure group's interests. Their influence is also seen by the fact that politicians are keen to get their support, and not upset them, especially in southern states like Arizona, where one politician was shot but still supports firearms use in America **g**.

ⓔ The third paragraph does well to **e** explore another area of pressure group influence, through judicial review. Although broad statements such as 'launched a number of cases against states and federal government' are too generalised to receive specific credit, the **f** explanation of the recent case in Washington DC, even if it does not specifically reference the 2008 *DC* v *Heller* case, does show enough knowledge to be given credit. In contrast, **g** the final point is not particularly well made, and the reference to the shooting of Gabrielle Giffords is not relevant either.

This shows the other way wealthy pressure groups can have more influence than poor groups, like the NAACP, by donating to candidate campaigns in order to get support for their interests, which is something poor groups can't afford to do **h**. Big US businesses like Wal-Mart can buy candidates' support and politicians are unwilling to go against pressure group donors when voting on issues. Previous regulations like the FECA and the recent McCain-Feingold financial reforms have not worked, as money always finds a way round regulations to help give more influence to wealthy pressure groups **i**. This was initially through PACs, where you could donate $5,000 to as many as you wanted, but more recently through 527s which are not restricted **j**. Thus wealthy pressure groups like the NRA have been able to set up lots of different PACs and 527s to influence politicians by giving them campaign money **k**.

ⓔ In this paragraph the student continues the unbalanced approach to the question by **h** explaining the impact of pressure group funding and **i j** showing a good knowledge of the regulations imposed on pressure group activities and the ways they have been circumvented through PACs and 527s. As is common with this topic, however, the student, in contrast to Student A, fails to give specific or detailed examples of where this has been used by wealthy groups to influence the system. Instead they revert to generalisations, with **k** claims like the 'NRA have been able to set up lots of different PACs and 527s to influence politicians'.

Another way they use their money is to gain insider influence with lobbying and the 'revolving door' **l**. Many wealthy pressure groups now invest millions in lobbying, and a whole industry has grown up in K Street in Washington **m**. This has meant that wealthy groups have been able to use their money to guarantee support from politicians and their advisers in order that they can get a job in the lobbying firm when they leave politics. Many leading politicians, such as one of Bush's cabinet, have taken up a role in lobbying firms with huge salaries, showing how they are able to influence the system with promises of well-paid jobs in the future **n**.

This is also linked to the 'iron triangle' theory, where wealthy pressure groups use their influence to support their interests. This is best seen with the influence of the major military contractors over the relevant congressional committee and with the federal bureaucracy. They all work together to keep US defence spending very high so weapons manufacturing pressure groups use this influence to secure contracts in return for campaign finance support of key members of the congressional committee. The existence of iron triangles shows how wealthy pressure groups can access the system to secure their own interests.

ⓔ These two paragraphs continue to present a solid case for the influence of wealthy pressure groups over those who are poor. Here they **l** show a good understanding of the development of insider status in advantaging wealthy groups and **m** present a good understanding of the influence of the lobbying industry. However, the response is again limited by the lack of detailed supporting evidence, as shown by **n** the broad example given of the 'revolving-door syndrome'. Similarly, this part of the essay fails to fully evaluate alternative arguments which might suggest that insider status and influence can be achieved even for poor pressure groups.

Overall, although some might say **o** that poor pressure groups do have a voice and can influence the system US, pressure groups have different levels of influence and it is true to say that money and wealth does ensure you are more powerful **p**. Poor pressure groups can't really affect the system as shown by Obama's limited healthcare reform. If these groups did have any power they would have ensured the wider coverage that they wanted to benefit the poor.

ⓔ Although the conclusion does attempt to address the synoptic element of the question, by **o** pointing out that 'some might say', this is too little, and too late, to be given any real credit. The student here uses the conclusion simply **p** to reaffirm their wholly unbalanced argument that wealth does give certain pressure groups an advantage. Overall, despite a generally good level of knowledge, this is a one-sided response. The answer as a whole would only just achieve a C grade in the exam.

AO1 KNOWLEDGE AND UNDERSTANDING: There are some good passages of knowledge, with most points having a degree of development, showing a sound understanding of the essay question. The student is also credited for their broad spread of knowledgeable points, especially those relating to **d** funding, **e** litigation and **l** lobbying.

AO2 EVALUATION AND ANALYSIS: This is a well-developed case, which looks at the influence wealthy pressure groups wield on the political system. However, the lack of a balanced argument restricts the student's ability to show a higher level of evaluation, which depresses the overall mark in this area.

SYNOPTICITY: The one-sided approach to the essay, which **c o** only hints at the debate over the question in the second and concluding paragraph, means the student has lost a considerable amount of marks in this area.

AO3 COMMUNICATION: The answer flows well enough and has a solid structure, making a series of clear points relevant to the question.

ⓔ **22/45 marks awarded:** 8/12 for AO1, 6/12 for AO2, 3/12 for synopticity, 5/9 for AO3.

Question 4 Racial and ethnic politics

To what extent is it true that equality remains a distant dream for most minority groups in the USA?

(45 marks)

(e) This question is asking whether or not minority groups, which would include African Americans, Latinos and Asians, have achieved true equality in America today. The use of the term 'To what extent' points towards the need for an evaluation of the evidence about *both* the political, social and economic opportunities for American minorities, *and* the evidence that they lack opportunities in these areas. Higher-level responses should be able to recognise and differentiate between the different experiences of equality among different ethnic and racial groups, rather than considering 'minority groups' as a cohesive body.

Student A

After the Supreme Court ruling of *Brown* v *Board of Education* the Supreme Court justices ruled the constitution to be 'colour blind', abolishing the Jim Crow laws and finally making the constitution support equality. Affirmative action was introduced to help ethnic minorities where they had in the past been overlooked **a**. However, the liberal argument remains that America is far from achieving racial equality **b**.

(e) Although this is a solid introduction, which **a** sets out the historical context and **b** relates this to the views of liberals, it could be improved by more clearly signposting the wider contemporary debate surrounding the question of equality, to secure synoptic marks.

In terms of political representation, ethnic minorities are relatively well represented in the House **c**. Although its make-up is not proportional to the different races in the country, racial equality in the House has come on a long way, with African Americans such as Georgia Representative Hank Johnson and Latino Illinois Representative Luis Gutierrez **d**. Similarly the Supreme Court can be seen as a melting pot of cultures, with newly elected Latino Justice Sonia Sotomayor and African American Justice Clarence Thomas **e**. The Senate, however, shows minorities, especially African Americans, to be very poorly represented with the only African American, Senator Roland Burrows for Illinois, losing his seat in the 2010 midterms **f**. Although there is better level of ethnic minority representation in the House, this does not necessarily show equality in America — many of these representatives come from especially created majority-minority districts such as Illinois' 4th district represented by Luis Guitierez or Chicago's 4th district, where 53.5% of the population are African American, represented by Hank Johnson. While those majority-minority districts do make the House more representative, the fact that voting districts have to be gerrymandered to enable ethnic minorities to get in to these positions suggests equality is still a distant dream **g**.

(e) The student uses the second paragraph to **c** evaluate the issue of political equality. They make excellent use of a wide range of very detailed examples to support their argument about the level of equality suggested by the level of political representation, among both African Americans and Latinos. Indeed they give a spread of examples, showing good depth of knowledge, from **d** the House, **e** the Supreme Court and **f** the Senate. The student uses the Senate example well to temper their judgement and set out the areas of ongoing inequality, as best evidenced by their concluding sentence **g** that the need for majority-minority districts suggests that the USA is still not fully equal.

> Much better representation is seen at state level with a number of predominantly white areas having African-American state legislatures. Jerry Green, for example, is an African-American state legislature in the 22nd district of New Jersey where more than 60% of the population is white. Similarly, in Colorado, African Americans make up less than 4% of the population yet the House and Senate have been led by two African Americans; Terence Carroll and Peter Groff **h**. The fact that ethnic minorities can win elections in these predominantly white areas suggests racial equality is much closer than some liberals believe, especially when one considers how supportive Colorado was of Jim Crow laws and slavery **i**.

ⓔ Again the student shows excellent depth of knowledge in **h** evaluating political representation at a state level, with a range of comprehensive examples. **i** This is well rounded up at the end of the paragraph, which links to the student's line of argument that there is more equality than some liberals might suggest.

> In terms of social and economic equality, figures clearly show that both African Americans and Latinos earn less, and are less likely to graduate college **j**. African Americans are on average more likely to go to prison than white people, and as a result of this nearly 13% of blacks cannot vote. However, other ethnic minorities such as Asians now almost match whites on employment, education and wage statistics, suggesting that the American political system is not, as some liberals would say, intrinsically racist. Indeed in a book 'no excuses' it claims that African Americans are further behind whites because of cultural issues **k**.

ⓔ This paragraph deals with the other criteria for measuring equality, namely social and economic, less well. It starts by summarising the problems faced, with **j** relevant but not particularly detailed examples. Similarly, though the student evaluates this by reviewing alternative evidence, this lacks the depth of knowledge shown earlier. Indeed the student could develop **k** the points, which effectively refer to model minorities, by specifying the evidence to support exactly how 'Asians now almost match whites', perhaps from the fact that in 2004 average earnings among Asian men were as high as $46,888.

> The view favoured by many conservatives, including African-American Supreme Court Justice Clarence Thomas, is that ethnic minorities should make no excuses. They argue that for genuine racial equality America must be a truly colour-blind society, meaning outlawing, as Arizona did in its 2010 midterm proposition **l**, affirmative action. For many, affirmative action is little more than 'positive racism', which, far from helping ethnic minorities, disadvantages them, making them lazy. This view is disputed by groups like the NAACP who push for more affirmative action believing it is the only way to ensure racial equality **m**.

e The fifth paragraph is also not as strong because it could be more clearly related to the question. Though it **l** sets out the conservative argument regarding equality, this drifts into the views of affirmative action. **m** The ending should look to explicitly link the points made earlier to the question set, and the student's judgement on how far this would suggest that equality was a 'distant dream'.

With America being a federal country it is difficult to say whether the country as a whole has equality or not. Many expect the 'liberal north' to be colour blind while the 'conservative south' is expected to still hold racist views, but this view is disputed by figures. For example Mississippi is a state in the Deep South which fought against the civil rights movement and is a state in which 36% of the population are ethnic minorities and yet it has 25% of the state legislature as ethnic minorities. Although this figure does show an under-representation of ethnic minorities, it is not as great as might be expected for a state which throughout the 1960s was regarded as racist **n**.

Overall it is clear that while America is not yet a country with complete equality, shown through the lack of African-American representation in the Senate, it has come a long way to achieving racial equality, with Barack Obama, an African American, holding the most powerful job in the country as president.

e The two final paragraphs show the strengths of this answer, which is an excellent attempt to engage with and evaluate the question set. The student's ability to **n** weigh up and evaluate evidence is shown at the end of the penultimate paragraph, where it explains what the evidence of state-level representation suggests about equality. The conclusion summarises the line of argument throughout. In an exam this very strong answer would achieve an A grade.

AO1 KNOWLEDGE AND UNDERSTANDING: An excellent range of examples shows substantial depth of knowledge on the level of political representation (especially points **d**, **e**, **f** & **h**). A more detailed understanding of the evidence surrounding social and economic equality (**j** & **k**) would secure an even higher mark in this area.

AO2 EVALUATION AND ANALYSIS: Although there is a very good level of evaluation regarding the issue of political equality throughout, the failure to fully develop an analysis of wider measures of equality somewhat limits the mark in this area.

SYNOPTICITY: This answer shows a good understanding of different interpretations on the question. However, further reference to the contemporary debate, such as in **b** the opening paragraph, and more explicit linkages to the question of (**l** & **m**) the conservative views shown in the fifth paragraph, could raise the synoptic marks further.

AO3 COMMUNICATION: Overall this is a very well-structured response, which fluently sets out the key points in separate paragraphs. The argument is well balanced but flows easily throughout the essay.

38/45 marks awarded: 10/12 for AO1, 9/12 for AO2, 10/12 for synopticity, 9/9 for AO3.

Student B

The USA was founded upon principles of freedom, liberty and equality, and until this day is recognised as the land of opportunity. However, fundamentally the constitution has undermined minority equality throughout history and particularly minority groups, such as Native Americans, still are perceived as 'second-class' citizens **a**. Initially, when the constitution was created, Article 1, section 2, clause 3 'excluded Indians' and classed African Americans as 'three fifths' of a person, thus creating a society in which equality is acceptable to only the 'majority' **b**.

Many conservatives would argue the last presidential election shows this dream, for black Americans, has been realised **c**. 2008 saw the election of Barack Obama, the first black president ever. Before this election in national government they would argue the presence of African Americans in positions of power shows equality of opportunity. Colin Powell and Condoleezza Rice are examples of this. Furthermore in the Supreme Court the emergence of the black Clarence Thomas adds to this argument **d**.

(e) The introduction **a** sets down the historical context to the question well and also relates this to the contemporary synoptic debate among **b** liberals, that equality is largely the preserve of the 'majority', and **c** conservatives, that political representation shows that the dream has been realised for all Americans. Although the student supports this second point well with relevant examples to show a degree of political representation, **d** these examples are somewhat broad, and certainly in the case of Powell and Rice quite dated. The student could easily have improved this by replacing these examples with more recent and detailed examples, such as those presented by Student A.

Despite claims from conservative supporters of theories such as 'no excuses' that racism no longer exists, many minorities view equality as a distant dream **e**.

(e) The student here makes a short but relevant point, which summarises the alternative argument and links well into the next paragraph. However, the point is not developed, with **e** no detail given on which conservative authors have proclaimed racism no longer exists or the basis for views that equality is a distant dream.

Within political institutions, minority groups are extremely under-represented, demonstrated through no African Americans in the Senate currently, and only three states only ever being held in history, despite comprising of 13% of the population **f**. However, conservatives point towards figures such as President Obama, Justice Clarence Thomas and Colorado's state president, who had positions of great power, to demonstrate that freedom of opportunity does exist **g**. Yet moderate liberals call for equality of outcome, as Bill Clinton famously described he wanted a cabinet which 'looked like America', only then shall equality be achieved. In contrast, in positions of power and responsibility, candidates cannot be appointed merely for equal representation, rather equality should not compromise ability and qualification **h**.

(e) This paragraph opens well, with **f** a relevant example regarding under-representation in the Senate. Again, however, the extent and accuracy of this knowledge is shown to be less thorough by the latter examples, given that **g** the first two of these are repeated from the second paragraph, while the third is wrong, probably referring to the fact that in 2008 both the State legislative chambers for Colorado were led by African Americans. Similarly, towards the end of this paragraph, the student **h** drifts from the question and makes quite a confused and poorly explained point regarding Clinton's administration and what appears to be a personal judgement not really related to the question.

> Since the civil rights movements in the 1960s and Supreme Court decisions such as *Brown* v *Board of Education* (1954), segregationist educational systems were illegal and methods such as bussing and quotas have been introduced as an attempt to create equality within education **i**. However, equality of outcome has not been achieved, with drop-out rates extremely high among Latino communities and minorities' lower representation in higher education. Moderate and pragmatic conservatives point towards the growing rate of African Americans graduating from high school, with currently 89% compared to 36% in the 1970s **j**.

ⓔ The fifth paragraph does not flow well from the preceding one and **i** merely sets out the historical context of the liberal argument, without initially making an analytical point. It does then draw back into the question with **j** a well-developed look at areas of ongoing educational inequality.

> This demonstrates that equality is slowly being achieved **k** and conservatives point towards the findings of 'no excuses' and achievements of model minorities such as Asians, whose graduation and average income exceeded those of whites in 2004, to indicate both the possibility of equality of outcome, which are no longer limited by social and inherent problems **l**.

ⓔ The concluding paragraph continues the student's argument that **k** there is general equality in the USA. **l** Again it points towards outline evidence for this among the Asian community, without presenting any specific or detailed evidence to reinforce the judgement. In fact the essay comes to an abrupt end and the student does not appear to have fully summarised the extent to which they agree with the question or the basis for that judgement. Overall this essay is a sound answer. It has some irrelevance, but largely focuses on the question, and would manage to get a C grade in the exam.

AO1 KNOWLEDGE AND UNDERSTANDING: Although there is some sound knowledge in places (such as points **d**, **f** & **j**), on the whole the knowledge is quite basic, with some points either lacking full development (as with **d**, **e** & **l**) or others being wrong or irrelevant (**g** & **h**).

AO2 EVALUATION AND ANALYSIS: The answer does attempt to address the question and present a balanced argument. However, the line of argument is not entirely clear while at times **h** it drifts away from the question.

SYNOPTICITY: Solid understanding of at least two views on the question, namely the liberal and conservative debate over the degree of equality, is shown.

AO3 COMMUNICATION: Although on the whole there is some structure to the answer, **i** the extent to which this flows throughout is limited. Similarly, the lack of a clear conclusion contributes to the loss of marks in this area.

23/45 marks awarded: 6/12 for AO1, 6/12 for AO2, 7/12 for synopticity, 4/9 for AO3.

LEARNING ZONE
COLEG CAMBRIA DEESIDE

Knowledge check answers

1 This is a system of government which divides power between the national (federal) government and the local (state) government. Under this system they each have separate lawmaking powers.

2 First-past-the-post is an electoral system in which the winner only needs to achieve a simple majority of the vote to win (one more vote than the nearest opponent). It is a winner-takes-all system, in that nothing is allocated to runners-up, unlike more proportional systems, which are based on the percentage of votes received.

3 Iowa is the first state to vote in the presidential nominating process, while New Hampshire holds the first primary. As a result, both the Iowa caucus and the New Hampshire primary receive huge amounts of attention from presidential nominees, as well as media coverage. Good or bad showings in these early elections can therefore make or break a candidate.

4 Pledged delegates are committed to vote for a certain candidate in the first ballot of votes, if that candidate is still in the race. Superdelegates are leading party figures who have not been committed to vote for a candidate in the primary process.

5 General elections occur every 2 years with all members of the House (2-year terms) and one-third of the Senate (6-year terms) facing re-election. The president is elected every 4 years, for a maximum of two terms.

6 Midterm elections are the congressional elections which take place midway through a president's term of office. During this time the entire House and one-third of the Senate are up for re-election.

7 Specific factions could include the moderate Tuesday Group or Main Street Republicans, while conservative groups could include the Tea Party Caucus or the Religious Right.

8 Pro-life views oppose abortion on moral grounds and advocate a legal ban. In contrast, pro-choice views advance a woman's legal right to terminate a pregnancy.

9 Try to be specific when mentioning groups and their influence within the parties by referring to particular factions. For the Republican Party, these could include the Tea Party Caucus; the Republican Tuesday Group; the Main Street Partnership. For the Democrats, groups would include the Congressional Progressive Caucus; the New Democrat Coalition; the Blue Dog Coalition.

10 The Electoral College is the institution established by the Founding Fathers to indirectly elect the president of the USA. Each state is given a certain number of electors, equal to the number of senators and representatives, who vote in their state capitals according to their election results. Currently, a candidate must receive over 270 Electoral College votes to secure the presidency.

11 The US political system separates the three main branches of government: the executive (President); the legislature (Congress); and the judiciary (Supreme Court). In addition to this, the powers of each branch overlap so that they hold each other to account, or check and balance each other. Thus, for example, the president nominates Supreme Court judges, but these are ratified by the Senate.

12 Under the Federal Election Campaign Act 1974, individual contributions to a candidate were limited to $1,000. Under the Bipartisan Campaign Reform Act 2002, the amount was raised to $2,000, but would increase with inflation.

13 'Hard money' refers to those contributions given directly to a candidate or their campaign team, limited to $2,000 under the BCRA. 'Soft money' refers to those unregulated funds given to national political parties, or unregulated independent organisations which are not directly linked to candidate campaigns, such as 527s.

14 There are a range of methods pressure groups can use to exert influence. These include collecting signatures to introduce a ballot initiative, and coordinating, funding or staffing a specific campaign.

15 As well as the Senate being one chamber of the legislature, meaning it is targeted because of its lawmaking role, it is also a target because of its foreign policy powers, its role in confirming appointments and the individual senator's filibuster powers.

16 Lobbying is the process whereby pressure groups aim to influence policy makers, which are usually lawmakers, through persuasion and the information they provide to those who need it.

17 The pressure group which funded *Brown* v *Board of Education* was the National Association for the Advancement of Colored People (NAACP).

18 Post-racial America is the view, which was particularly prevalent following Obama's election to the presidency, that race is no longer an issue in the USA. The political, economic and social achievements of minorities have been used as evidence that race is no longer a barrier to success.

19 Conservatives believe in equality of opportunity, which is guaranteed by ensuring all races and ethnic groups are free from discrimination, and thus have the same chances as whites. Liberals, however, believe in equality of outcome and would point to the existence of lingering institutional racism which, despite legal protection against racism and discrimination, results in ongoing disadvantages for minority groups.

20 Restrictions in affirmative action have come through Supreme Court decisions which have limited the scope of its programmes and through a series of initiatives and propositions which have banned its use across some states.

21 In 2003 the *Gratz* v *Bollinger* case declared the University of Michigan's racial quota system of admissions unconstitutional as it was 'too mechanistic'. In contrast, the *Grutter* v *Bollinger* case upheld the UCLA's Law School admissions policy, with its more 'individualised' approach to affirmative action.